The Way of the Horned God

A Young Man's Guide
to Modern Paganism

First published by Moon Books, 2010
Moon Books is an imprint of John Hunt Publishing Ltd., Laurel House, Station Approach,
Alresford, Hants, SO24 9JH, UK
office1@jhpbooks.net
www.johnhuntpublishing.com
www.moon-books.net

For distributor details and how to order please visit the 'Ordering' section on our website.

Text copyright: Dancing Rabbit 2009

ISBN: 978 1 84694 267 9

A CIP catalogue record for this book is available from the British Library.

Design: Stuart Davies

Printed and bound by CPI Group (UK) Ltd, Croydon, CR0 4YY

We operate a distinctive and ethical publishing philosophy in all
areas of our business, from our global network of authors to
production and worldwide distribution.

The Way of the Horned God

A Young Man's Guide
to Modern Paganism

Dancing Rabbit

Illustrated by W. Michael Dooley

MOON
BOOKS

Winchester, UK
Washington, USA

CONTENTS

Acknowledgements

I'd like to acknowledge all the folks who helped out in some way with the writing of this book: my friends who proofread the manuscript, caught my typos, and gave me their advice on style and content: Jeffry Downs, Rev. Adam Robinson, Jennifer Ramon, Alex de la Fuente, Christopher Pinkston, Nick Miller, Bill Kunkle, Fire Eagle, Nigh, Wyrmwood, Paul Miller and Ravenlore, and John Hunt and the folks at O-Books for publishing it.

Dedications

To my wife, Cindy, who encouraged me to keep writing, gave me the space to write and was patient when I insisted in re-writing yet again and to the Rev. Gail Lindsey-Marriner who helped me through some of the darkest times in my life and taught me so much about how to encounter the sacred in my life, and to the Rev. Jose Ballester who taught me by his example of spirituality through social justice and whose worship services were always full of fun and hope.

Dancing Rabbit was born in the small mill town of Crossett, Arkansas on September 20, 1952. He holds a MEd degree and has taught in public school for 23 years. He began learning about and practicing Paganism in 1993 and is co-facilitator of Rhythm of Life Chalice Circle. He has written several articles on experiential education. This is his first book on Pagan spirituality. He currently lives in Houston Texas with his wife Cindy, his Basenjis Bell, Ra and Shango, and his bunny Trickster.

W. Michael Dooley is a professional illustrator and artist and is widely known in the furry community for his anthropo-morphic art. He was one of the illustrators for the book *The Urban Primitive*.

Preface

The eight-year-old boy was puzzled. In his first years of Sunday school at the First Unitarian Congregation of Ottawa, Ontario, he'd surely noticed the attention paid to women's rights. But on this morning, the feminist message was especially robust. It was International Women's Day, after all, and his teachers were impassioned as they led students in naming women leaders, women heroes, and the court cases that had brought equal rights to Canadian women. Finally, the puzzled boy spoke his mind. "This feminism stuff is interesting," he told his teachers, "but when are we going to have a class on boyism?"[1]

    Rev. Neil Chethik

Why I wrote this book...

When ARE we going to have a class on "boyism"? This is not just a Canadian or a Unitarian problem. Look at the bookshelves down at the local Pagan/New Age bookstore. There are shelves of books that deal with the Goddess and woman's spirituality, even a few written especially for Pagan girls but very little specifically for men and almost nothing for Pagan boys. Why? Maybe it's the market: females buy more of this sort of thing than we males do. Maybe it's in the nature of modern Paganism that places a renewed emphasis on the Goddess. Perhaps the paradigm has finally shifted away from patriarchy toward matriarchy. In any case, it seems there is little out there specifically for boys or men.

    I had just finished reading *The Goddess in Every Girl* by M. J. Abadie and felt that someone should do something about the lack of books for young Pagan men. Since it didn't look like anyone else was going to, I decided to try my hand at it. I had been working on this book for about a year when, while browsing through the books at The Magick Cauldron, I saw *Sons of the Goddess* by Christopher Penczak. My first thought was,

1

"Oh, no! I've been scooped. That's my book, the one I should have hurried up and written." I thought about giving up then and there but then I realized there is more than one book out on almost every subject. Maybe what I had to say would be sufficiently different to justify the effort of writing. I decided go ahead with the project. I didn't read *Sons of the Goddess* until after I finished writing and sure enough we had written quite different books. Even where we deal with the same topics, we approach them out of our own personal experience, so they are different. If you have not yet read his book, I highly recommend it.

To the parent...

If you are Pagan, I hope you will find this book useful in helping your son grow up to be a man who will be responsible, courageous and kind, a true Son of the Great Goddess and the Horned God. I hope you will read it so you can help him in his quest for manhood.

If you are not Pagan, I hope that this will ease your fears that your son has gotten involved in some kind of destructive cult. I hope this book will help you understand the spiritual path he has chosen for himself and even though you would not choose it for yourself, at least, you will come to understand why he did.

To the young man...

Perhaps you have already been practicing Paganism for some time. As you read this book take what is useful and add it to what you are already doing. If you are new to Paganism, as you read, know that this is primarily a religion of doing, rather than believing. The only way to understand it is to experience it. So don't just read. Do. We males are naturally more inclined to doing things rather than just sitting around and talking about them anyway.

There are a lot of reasons people are drawn to Paganism, some good, some not so good. Paganism is not a fashion statement, a clique or scene to join, a way to be really weird at school, a way to drive your parents crazy or to learn a lot of spells and get powerful. If you seek the Horned God for those reasons, you will be disappointed. If, however, you are a young man who is interested in working toward harmony within yourself and with nature then this book is written especially for you. So, introduction over, let's get on with it!

Chapter 1

Beginning Your Pagan Journey

Spirit of the cloven hoof is running wild on the land
Spirit of the cloven hoof is running wild on the land
Horned God of this land I call to you, I call to you
Horned God of this land I call to you, I call to you
Pan, Herne, Cernunnous, Pan, Herne, Cernunnous
Jana Runnalls[2]

Paganism

What is Paganism? The word has several different related meanings but let's look at how I'm going to use the word in this book. Paganism is a term for the various pre-Christian earth centered religions of Western Europe and those modern religions based on them. As Christianity expanded across Europe it was first accepted in the cities by the educated, literate people. People who lived in the more rural parts of the Roman Empire and continued to practice their pre-Christian religions were called *paganus*, meaning country folk or hicks. The Christian Church dealt with Paganism in two different ways. Early on, Pagan deities, traditions and shrines were absorbed into the Christian faith so Pagans could become Christians without giving up their folk culture. Churches were built on the sites of Pagan temples, Pagan deities became Christian saints and Pagan holidays were given Christian names. For example: Christmas, the birthday of the Son of God in the Christian religion was set at about the same date as Winter Solstice, the birthday of the Roman Sun God. Most of the present day Christmas folk customs like evergreen trees, holly, reindeer and mistletoe have nothing to do with the birth of Jesus of Nazareth and everything to do with pre-

5

Christian Pagan religion. As the church gained political power, Pagans were persecuted along with Jews, heretical Christians and an assortment of other people who were unlucky enough be perceived as a threat. The old Pagan religions died away – but not out. What survived were some of the superstitions and folk customs.

Today, Neopaganism (new Paganism) is comprised of those newly created earth centered religions loosely based on what is remembered of the pre-Christian religions of Western Europe. Some people criticize the new Paganism as being a "made-up religion" but when you think about it, every religion was made up by people at some time back in history and has been changed by people over time to meet their changing needs. The particular kind of Neopaganism I follow, just so you know where I'm coming from, is eclectic. I have borrowed mainly from Wicca with a heavy dose of Humanism thrown in. I am a member of a Unitarian Universalist Church and consider that my spiritual home.

As you study and begin to walk the earth centered path of Pagan spirituality you will learn the myths, the rituals and the practical applications of the religion. People often use the word "myth" to mean an idea that is not true or a story that is pure fantasy. This is not what I mean by the word. Myths are stories that give you insight into sacred truths that can't be told in ordinary language. They are more than just old campfire stories. By using symbolic language, they are a way to understand the universe and your place in it. Rituals are a series of symbolic actions that act out the myths. Most of the ritual that we modern people have experience with is what I call dead ritual, just going through the motions of something that doesn't have any meaning for us. The main reason that ritual becomes ineffective is that it is done in the absence of the myth that it celebrates. Our ancestors did not do ritual just have something exciting to do. They were acting out the central myths of their time. Paganism is not just doing rituals or casting spells. It is about using ritual to act out your myths and thus make real changes in yourself and your world. It is immanently practical. When our ancestors had completed a hunting ritual they left the circle of the campfire and went on the hunt. They didn't sit around expecting wild game to just magickally drop into their circle. They did expect the re-enactment of the myth in ritual to aid them in the hunt. You too will learn to use Pagan myth and ritual to aid you in living life in the postmodern world.

Parental Issues

It would be nice if every young man who was beginning to explore Paganism had nice supportive Pagan parents but since most people aren't Pagan it follows that most parents aren't either. Hopefully, your parents will respect your choice of spiritual path. Hopefully, you can come out to them and they will at least tolerate your religion. If you feel that they would react badly to your announcement, what are you, the serious young Pagan, to do? You need to understand why your parents feel as they do. This is a first step toward finding a way to do something about it or at least live with it.

What are the reasons your parent might object to your exploration and practice of Pagan spirituality? Maybe they are the sort of fundamentalists who sincerely believe that their religion is the only TRUE religion and that all others are satanic and evil. Maybe they just hope that their child will stay within the family religious tradition and are disappointed that you want to try something else. Maybe they aren't concerned that you are going to lose your soul and burn in hell but are just concerned that you are getting involved with some kind of cult that is going to take advantage of you and warp your mind. They basically just want what they perceive is best for you. If there is a key to solving this dilemma, it is for you to understand where they are coming from and for them to understand what your spiritual path is really about.

On the surface you have at least three options as to what to do. You can put off practicing your religion until you turn 18 and get out on your own. You can be totally open about what you are doing from the start, or you can practice your spirituality in secret with the chance that your secret may be discovered. What you do is your choice and you should spend some time thinking about it.

The consequences of the first choice are pretty obvious. Those of the second will depend on your parents and how you go about telling them. If you decide to take the third course of action and practice in secret, no matter how well you hide your stash of Pagan stuff (Book of Shadows, ritual tools, spell components, etc.) chances are that sooner or later your parents will find it. The better the hiding place and the bigger the lock on your box of Pagan stuff, the more upset your parents will be when they do find it. The same goes for whatever rituals you perform. Sooner or later they are going to either walk in on you or wonder what you are doing behind locked doors especially if there are all sorts of odd sounds and smells involved. Even if they don't discover what you are up to, you are building yet another barrier between you and your parents, and taking on negative energy in the process.

Let me suggest a less apparent fourth path if you decide that you can not be open about what you are doing and do not want to wait. Do what folks who practiced Paganism during times when discovery by the authorities meant torture and death did. Practice openly but not obviously.

Pagans during times of persecution didn't worship in marble temples with special ritual equipment. They met in ordinary places: in the woods where they hunted, in fields where they grew their crops or in the home of someone who was trusted. Space was consecrated and a magick circle visualized or traced on the ground in a way that could be quickly erased. Ritual tools were ordinary household items like a broom, walking stick, knife or cooking pot. The candles they used in spells didn't look any different from the ones that they used to light their homes. The herbs they used were spices they used in cooking and for first aid. Their deity statue might be made of straw or wax and could be quickly tossed in the fireplace if the authorities burst through the door.

Times have changed. Hooded cloaks and iron cauldrons aren't part of daily life, but there are a variety of ways you can practice your religion more or less openly without anyone realizing that what you are doing is a religion at all. This would allow you to begin practicing your religion now rather than waiting until you are an adult and without suffering major hassles from your parents. More importantly, it would allow you to let your parents see you practicing Paganism without realizing that is what they are looking at. That way when they do find out or you decide to tell them it isn't such a shock. They will have seen you DOING Paganism for years and have seen that it isn't something strange and spooky. It is instead something very positive and totally natural. This fourth option is only temporary. The ultimate goal is to be able to talk to your parents about your chosen faith.

If despite your best efforts and intentions they insist that you are worshiping the devil and are damned for all eternity, the best you can do is to accept that this is what they believe. It is one thing to show or explain. It is another to debate or argue. Don't let them draw you into their battles. Use "I" statements rather than "You" statements. Such as, "I understand you believe this very strongly", "I am sorry this upsets you", "I know that you love me and have my best interests at heart", "I will be glad to answer your questions when we can talk calmly". Stand your ground but remember the first one to lose their temper loses.

Pagan Ethics

Ethics is that branch of philosophy that has to do with right and wrong, good and evil. How do you decide if something is right or wrong? Is it always wrong or does it depend on the circumstances? What is good? What is evil? Unlike some religions that have a list of specific rules given by God or a religious leader, Paganism has one very general principal called The Rede. "An' it harm none, do as ye will." Pagans aren't bound by a list of do's and don'ts. That doesn't mean we can do anything we feel like doing, though. If it harms someone, including yourself, don't do it. If you do anyway then there are consequences.

What if you do something that harms someone else? You should apologize to them and if it's possible make it right. Then don't do it again. Simple. You take responsibility for your actions. There is no feeling guilty and going to a god for forgiveness. You go to the person you offended. Only you can do something about your own actions. Our Gods don't expect a sacrifice, just responsibility. If someone hurts you then you may protect yourself. You may not take revenge and try to harm them in return. You are not required to forgive them but you will want to do something to turn loose of the negative feelings you have so you won't be carrying them around all the time. Harming none also means not doing things that harm yourself. This includes things that obviously harm you but also things in excess. There's nothing wrong with drinking a soda but if you drink a liter or two a day there might be.

Pagans view "good" as a state of being in balance and harmony with one's self, with others and with the world around you. Light and dark are not symbols of good and evil for us. A day is made up of both daylight and darkness. It would be really bad if there were only daytime and no night, ever. Summer and winter are both part of the whole year. Even death is not evil. It's a natural part of the cycle of life. Evil is when things get out of balance.

Since Pagans view everything as connected to everything else, the effects of your actions come back to you. This is called the

Law of Return or the Three-fold Law. It's the idea that you reap what you sow. Some people call it karma. Things you do have an effect and the ripples of your actions come back to you. Sometimes it's just that your actions change who you are. In any case, there is no vengeful deity keeping track of your misdeeds and getting ready to punish you. Your deeds create their own reward or punishment. So it's up to you to take responsibility for your own actions.

Your Book of Shadows

Paganism is not a revealed religion like Judaism, Christianity, or Islam in which God reveals his words to a prophet who shares them with us ordinary mortals, directly or in a holy book. Paganism is a natural religion. Every Pagan has direct access to the deities. So don't use this book or any other book as if it were Holy Scripture. It isn't. Hopefully it contains some truths and will help you discover more truths but it isn't The Truth.

Paganism is about walking a path that brings you into harmony with yourself and others by living in harmony with the cycles of nature. It is about reconnecting with the divine energy inside you, the divine energy in nature, and the divine energy in other people. It is about the free and responsible search for truth and meaning.[3] It is a path that you have to discover by walking it and not by reading about it or being told about it. This, and many other books, can be useful roadmaps but they aren't the road itself.

Most Pagans do keep personal journals that include prayers, chants, spells, rituals, various formulae and other information they find useful. This spiritual diary is called a Book of Light and Shadows, or just a Book of Shadows. This is not just a spooky name for a journal but was a term originated by Gerald Gardner, one of the first modern Pagans go public. The name represents how Pagans view light and dark, day and night, not as dualistic enemies but as a polarity, as two sides of the same coin. Dark is not evil. Light is not good. A day is made up of both daytime and nighttime. The year is made up of both summer and winter. Both are necessary and good in balance. Your Book of Shadows is your daily spiritual diary documenting your journey toward that harmony.

Organized groups and traditions usually have a coven or traditional Book of Shadows but these books should not be treated as inspired scriptures either. Rather they should be considered collections of information useful to the group. If you have been involved in Paganism for some time and have started writing your Book of Shadows, you might skip the rest of this section.

You don't need an expensive witchy-looking hardbound book. This would be a waste of money and would just attract attention. I suggest you buy a ring binder like you would use at school. It's cheap, flexible, ordinary looking and portable. Divide your Book of Shadows into sections so that you can find things easily, though I wouldn't put Pagan terms on the divider tabs. Rather than listing it as Diary, Myths, Rituals, Spells, Chants and so forth, consider labeling the tabs something like: Journal, Stories, Scripts, Songs, Recipes and Projects.

However, this is the 21st century and doing your Book of Shadows on your computer and saving it to a CD or flash drive may be both easier and more secure. Whatever works best for you. If other people use your computer, be aware that most word processor programs keep a history of recent files and that web browsers also keeps a file of your documents in their History File. You should clear these to keep your private writing private. However, going to the trouble of encrypting your files is a little like using a magical alphabet or writing in code. Your file may be so well encrypted that you can not read it later on, and since it looks strange it just attracts unwanted attention.

Your Book of Shadows is private, like a diary. There are people who have very negative attitudes toward Paganism whom you definitely don't want reading it because of how they might then act towards you. Keep it put up without actually hiding it. Make it as ordinary looking as possible. The original Pagans, if they wrote anything down at all, didn't have the spare money to buy something exotic looking. They used whatever material they had available.

So, your first project is to begin your Book of Shadows. Make your first journal entry. What have you done so far? What do you find attractive about Paganism? How did you discover it? What are your concerns, your plans, your feelings, your hopes and your fears?

Chapter 2

Encountering the Sacred

The holy is nothing but the ordinary, held up to the light and profoundly seen. It is the awareness of creativity and a connection that we do not control, in a universe that is always larger, more intricate, and more astonishing than we imagine. It is the acknowledgement that we are formed by the earth from which we arise, and in which we live and move and have our being; and that we are, finally not alone.[4]

Rev. Kendyl Gibbons

What is the Sacred?

In western patriarchal religions, the world is divided into the sacred that pertains to God and spiritual things, and the profane that has to do with the physical universe that we can perceive through our senses. The profane is fallen, sinful and evil. Earth is not our home. We are just passing through on the way to heaven or hell. So it's OK to dominate and use our planet and the life upon it. The joys and pleasures of our physical bodies are sinful, to be avoided and atoned for. The sacred is something separate from the physical universe that we are supposed to worship and aspire to. God alone is holy and worthy of worship.

The Sacred or Holy is, for us, that which inspires awe and reverence, that which we should treat with respect, that which we worship. For Pagans, it is the physical world all around us that we experience through our senses. There is no sharp division between the sacred and the profane, the spiritual and the physical, the religious and the mundane. Because Paganism is a nature religion, the Earth and all life upon it, including your own, is sacred. The Sun, the moon, the stars and the planets are sacred. I don't *believe* in the Gods any more than I believe in the Sun or the moon or the rocks or the cycle of the seasons. I don't believe in them. I experience Them in my daily life. I connect with the Gods by connecting with nature because I believe that nature is sacred. I worship Them when I show respect for "the interdependent web of all existence of which we are a part."[5]

Although I live in a large city, I try to go out into nature as often as possible, whether it's walking in the woods or along the beach. I also show my reverence for nature by picking up litter along my street, walking instead of driving to the store, recycling, and using wind and solar-generated electricity. I compost the leaves and grass clippings rather than burning them or throwing them away. I enjoy working in my garden. For me, these too are acts of worship.

As a Pagan, I not only see nature as sacred. I see myself as a part of the sacred because I am not separate from nature but a part of it. I am a child of the Goddess and the Horned God. They are not distant beings living in heaven or some other plane of existence but are as close as my own breath. The same force that lives in the universe also lives in me. I therefore see the qualities and roles of both the Goddess and the Horned God in me.

Some western Pagans have adopted the Hindu greeting "namaste" which literally means "I bow to you" but more fully implies "I honor and worship the holy within you." The greeting is made by bringing the palms of the hands together at chest level, fingers pointed up, while bowing slightly. I don't often say the word or make the gesture of namaste around people who are not Pagans because most of them would either not understand or misunderstand what I was doing. I do try to see the Holy within the people I encounter.

People who have lost touch with the holiness of nature have also lost touch with the holiness within themselves and within their fellow human beings. A Holy God who is separate from the fallen and evil material universe makes sense to them. He is a strict father who is angry with his children and demands blood sacrifice or punishment. Our Pagan Gods are Nature itself. We worship Gods who are our nurturing parents and who expect us to, as part of growing up, take responsibility for our actions. They can be seen in the cycles of the moon and the Sun and the stars. Since we humans are part of nature, we too have the Holy within each of us. Our Gods can be seen in the cycles of our own lives. We can find our Gods in the circle of friends and family around the 'campfire'. We know that we all have an "inherent worth and dignity."[6]

Paganism is about living your daily life harmoniously. Life is sacred and the natural world is Holy. Although we usually experience the world through our logical conscious minds, I believe that we can also experience it through what I call ritual consciousness. Our conscious mind is logical and linear and tied to words, language. It's that voice chattering away in your head. In Pagan worship we use ritual to still the conscious mind so that we can experience the world directly through our senses as we did when we were very young children. In this state of ritual consciousness we experience the sacred both inside us and in the world around us directly.

Centering and Grounding

I prepare to meet the Sacred through centering and grounding. Centering involves focusing your thoughts on the center of your being and so that you are truly here and now. It involves being aware of how you are feeling right now. As stray thoughts come into your mind, acknowledge them and let them go. Don't think them for long but don't get impatient that they come through your mind. Breathe deeply and slowly and allow your mind to become quiet as you focus on a spot an inch or two below where your ribs come together. This spot is called the solar plexus. It is where the nerves that control breathing join together in a sort of knot of nerves or ganglion.

Grounding involves recognizing your connection to the Earth. At the beginning of a ritual, pay attention to the feeling of your feet pressing against the ground. Visualize roots growing out the bottoms of your feet and down into the Earth. Imagine energy flowing up like sap in a great tree. At the end of a ritual, place your hands on the ground palm down and visualize energy flowing through your arms, into your hands and back down into the Earth.

Grounding and centering don't always have to be closed-eyed meditations. You can center yourself with your eyes wide open. Notice the sights and sounds around you. Acknowledge them and then shift your attention to your center. You can remain centered while paying attention to what is going on around you. This is called Mindful Mediation or just Mindfulness.

As you are finding your center, let your gaze move slowly taking in the details of things around you. Listen to the sounds without focusing on one to the exclusion of others. Take them all in hearing them all. Breathing deeply and being aware of the smells in the air. As you walk pay attention to your feet touching the ground, to the feeling of the Earth under your feet. You can do this while you are walking down the street or waiting for the light to change, when you are working in your garden or cleaning your room.

In Mindfulness, you are focused on what you are doing in a detached sort of way. You are not zoned out or daydreaming but are focused on the information coming in through your senses right at that moment. You should ground and center at the beginning and end of rituals. You can also use the techniques by themselves.

As you work through this book, you will be doing and creating Pagan rituals. You will therefore need to find and prepare safe places to do them. Let's first look at indoor locations and then later at the outdoor ones.

Indoor Sacred Places

When I speak of "sacred space" or a "sacred place" I don't mean to imply that you are going to make a space sacred or that one place is more or less sacred than another. What you are going to do is create a space where you can meet or acknowledge the Sacred. It is possible to create sacred space almost anywhere you are. If you are going to do an elaborate ritual you will need some privacy. This is where the need to find a sacred place comes in. A sacred place for me is a place where I often go to create sacred space because of its beauty or privacy.

What room in the house is more or less exclusively, privately, yours? Unless you share it with a brother, it's your bedroom. Stand at the doorway to your bedroom and look in. Is it neat and orderly or is it cluttered and chaotic? Does it smell clean and fresh or does it smell more like a toxic waste dump? The physical appearance of your main working space has a huge effect on the work you do in it. Your sacred place should be physically what you want your spiritual life to be like.

To prepare your room for use as your indoor sacred place, you will need the following items: a large trash bag, broom or vacuum cleaner if your room is carpeted, a bucket of water, a mop (unless your room is carpeted), a cloth, a roll of paper towels, 3 lemons, a knife, a small candle and holder, some lavender incense and holder, a small bowl of water, a small bowl with about a spoonful of salt and some matches. Put the last 5 items on a shelf or somewhere they will not be in plain view.

First, the physical work: Take a large trash bag and pick up the obvious trash like that empty soda bottle in the corner and that pizza box under the bed. There may be other things lying about that aren't exactly trash but should be trashed. Strip your bed and take the sheets and any other dirty clothes to the laundry room. If you don't know how to run the washer, now would be a good time to learn so that you aren't just creating a pile of work for your parents to do. Next, start putting things in their place: books on the bookshelf and clean clothes in the closet or dresser. Find a place for things or throw them out. No, under the bed is not a "place".

Next cut one of the lemons in half and squeeze the juice into the bucket of water. Drop the lemon halves in too. With your right hand stir it deosil (clockwise in the northern hemisphere, counterclockwise in the southern hemisphere) imagining the fresh cleansing energy of the lemon swirling round in the water.

Sweep or vacuum the floor. If your floor is not carpeted, use the lemon water to mop your floor. If your room is carpeted, after you vacuum sprinkle a small amount of lemon water (not enough to get the carpet soggy) about and imagine the sunny energy of the lemon cleansing your carpet. Pour the dirty water out and imagine the negative crud from your room going down the drain. Prepare a second bucket of lemon water and dip the cloth in it and wring it until it is almost dry. Use the damp cloth to dust the shelves and tabletops as you go. With a third bucket of lemon water and paper towels, wash your windows. Pour out the last of the water, take out the trash, put your cleaning supplies away, make your bed, look around your room and see if there is anything you have missed. Is your desk neat or is it still a pile of clutter? What about the closet? Well, maybe next time.

Now, the ritual: Close and lock your door and put the 5 items that you previously set aside on your desk or a small table. Put the bowl of salt to the north, the incense to the east, the candle to the south and the bowl of water to the west. Light the candle and the incense. Stand up straight, close your eyes and take three deep slow breaths. Acknowledge the thoughts that are running through your mind and turn your attention to the center of your body just below where your ribs come together. Relax. Imagine roots growing downwards from your feet into the earth. Feel energy flowing up from the earth into your body like sap in a tree. Imagine a line of glowing silvery light tracing its way deosil around your room beginning at the east and going round until it forms a circle.

Open your eyes. Face east, extend your right hand as if you are waving to someone in the distance and say, "Spirits of the East and of Air, guard, guide and protect my circle." Close all but your index finger and trace a five-point star in the air starting at the top point and moving first to the lower left. Then trace a circle around it deosil. Face south and using a similar gesture say, "Spirits of the South and of Fire, guard, guide and protect my circle." Then turn to the west and say, "Spirits of the West and of Water, guard, guide and protect my circle." Finally, turn to the north and say, "Spirits of the North and of Earth, guard, guide and protect my circle." Now extend both arms upwards and outwards like a small child reaching up to his mother. Close your hands into a loose fist and then open your index finger and thumb to form two crescents. (This is the Goddess position.) Say, "Lovely Lady, guard, guide and protect my circle." Bring your arms down so that they are crossed over your chest, like King Tut, then holding your middle two fingers closed with your thumb extend your index and little finger. (This is the Horned God position.) Say, "Laughing Lord, guard, guide and protect my circle."

Pick up the incense with your power hand (right if you are right-handed, left if you are left-handed) and walk slowly around your room deosil saying these or words similar, "I bless this, my room, by air. By air be clean." Pick up the candle with your right hand and walk slowly around your room in the same direction saying, "I bless this, my room, by fire. By fire be clean." Pick up the bowl of water with your left hand and walk round your room as before dipping the fingers of your right hand into the water and sprinkling a little of it as you go, saying, "I bless this, my room, by water. By water be clean." Pick up the bowl of salt with your left hand and walk round your room sprinkling a little salt as you go, saying, "I bless this, my room, by earth. By earth be clean."

Stand near the center of your room, close your eyes and take a deep, slow breath, assume the Goddess position and say, "Lovely Lady, bless this, my room. May it be clean." Take another deep slow breath, assume the Horned God position and say, "Laughing Lord, bless this, my room. May it be clean." Relax and imagine energy flowing up from the earth through your feet, up your legs and into your body. Extend your arms outward, hand open, palms out and tense all your muscles for a moment.

Imagine energy radiating outward cleansing and empowering your room.

As the energy flows outward, relax again and take a deep slow breath, saying, "My Lord and my Lady, thank you for your presence here. Thank you that my room is now clean. May there ever be peace between us. Spirits of the East, South, West and North, thank you for your presence here. Thank you that my room is now clean. May there ever be peace between us." Imagine the glowing circle of light fading and moving outward like a ripple on a smooth pond. Now say, "The circle is open yet unbroken. Merry meet and merry part and merry meet again." Breathe slowly and deeply. Sink down to the floor in a sitting or kneeling position and put the palms of your hands flat on the floor. As you breathe out, imagine energy flowing down your arms, through your hands and into the ground, and say, "My rite is ended. Blessed be."

Extinguish the candle. Some people prefer to use a candle snuffer or to pinch out the candle with their fingers. They feel this is more respectful. I prefer to just blow the candle out with the image in mind of my breath blowing the energy of the candle out into the universe. You can either extinguish the incense or let it burn out. Pour the salt and the water down the drain, wash the dishes you have used and put them away. Before you go on to do something else, let's look back at what you did and why.

First you did the physical half of the work. Then you centered and grounded, shifting into ritual consciousness. You cast a magick circle around yourself to mark the space in which you would meet the Sacred. You invited spirits of the Elements, the Goddess, and the Horned God into your space. You cleansed and charged the space with the four Elements and asked the Goddess and the Horned God to bless it. You raised power and directed it outward to cleanse and empower your room. Having finished the ritual, you thanked and said farewell to the Elements and the Deities, released your magick circle and grounded any excess energy. Lastly, you put away the physical tools you used in your ritual and took a moment to review how the ritual had gone.

Unless you are a confirmed neat freak, you don't have to keep your room in perfect order at all times. You may choose to but it's not a requirement. It is important to give it a good cleansing once a month or so, preferably during the Waning Moon.

Your altar

When you did your room blessing ritual, you put salt, incense, a candle and water on a working surface. This was your altar for that ritual. That's really all an altar is, a working surface that you've dedicated for ritual use. An altar doesn't have to be some kind of permanent shrine. An altar can be temporary; something that you can set up to do a ritual and take down after you finish.

The simplest sort of altar would involve just a cloth, a colored handkerchief or bandana that you would use to cover your working surface. When you place your altar cloth on a desk or table or the floor or the ground, it becomes your altar. Choose a color that appeals to you or one that corresponds to the season, the time of the moon or the sort of magick you plan to do.

The next step up would be to have a small table that you could dedicate exclusively for use as your altar. While you will want to put the things that you would actually use in a ritual away when you aren't using them, there are lots of decorative items that you could put on your altar that most people wouldn't recognize as being Pagan. They would just assume that it was some artful seasonal decoration: flowers in the spring, greenery in summer, an arrangement of fruit and fall leaves in autumn, or evergreens in winter.

An outdoor altar is also something that you set up and take down. You can use what happens to be there: a tree stump or a flat rock. If nothing seems altar-like at the place you've chosen, you could bring your altar with you and carry home when you are done. A small wooden box can serve a dual purpose. It can be used to carry the things you need for that particular ritual and by covering it with a cloth become your altar.

Before you use your altar the first time you should to do a ritual to cleanse and dedicate it. The ritual that you used to cleanse your room would work nicely substituting the words, "my altar" for "my room" of course.

Sometimes I put physical representations of the four Elements on my altar. On the North I put a dish of salt for Earth, on the East, incense for Air, on the South a candle for Fire and on the West a small bowl of water for Water. Other times I use a colored votive candle to represent the directions: green for North, yellow for East, red for South and blue for West. There are traditions that use different colors schemes. This is the one I use.

Your tools

Most books on Paganism might lead you to believe that you must have an official set of altar tools: an athame (knife), wand, cup and pentacle. These tools are like the costumes and props that help make a good play better. They make doing ritual a little easier and more fun, however, the most powerful ritual tool you have is your mind. If you don't know how to use it, a whole Pagan store full of ritual tools won't help you do ritual.

I use my athame or black handled knife as the tool of the Element of Air, the East, and the intellect. The image is of a sharp mind cutting through mental fog and confusion. I use my athame to project energy when I'm casting a circle or blessing an object. If you can't go out and buy a small dagger and have it in your room without raising suspicions, I have two possible solutions. You can to buy an inexpensive table knife and paint the handle black. If even that would arouse suspicion then simply use your right or dominant hand. Hold it open with your fingers together in what's called a knife hand position. It doesn't matter that your hand is not sharp. Your ritual knife isn't going to be cutting anything tougher than air anyway.

I use my wand as the tool of the Element of Fire, the South and the will. The image is of a magick wand shooting fire from its tip or of a scepter as a symbol of authority. Like the athame, it is used in projective magick. I use it when I'm planting seeds and when I am blessing a person. A wooden dowel or tree branch as thick as of your index finger makes a good wand. Some traditions say that a person's wand should be cut the length from finger tips to elbow but that makes it a bit long to be easily hidden. I have one that I've had since I started practicing Paganism that is thirteen inches long, a length that works very well for me. I've seen wands in Pagan shops that are decorated with stones, crystals and wire wrapping. Personally, I like simple but if you are attracted to something more elaborate there is nothing wrong with it.

I also have a staff or walking stick that I sometimes use for the same purpose as a wand. If you don't happen to have your wand with you or having one would arouse suspicion then use your right or dominant hand and point with your index finger. Some traditions use the wand to represent the East and intellect and the athame to represent the South and will. There is nothing wrong in this. If the other works for you, go for it. I use the tradition that I learned first and that works for me.

The cup is the tool of the Element of Water, the West and emotion. The image is of a cup receiving and holding emotions which are fluid and changeable. It is used in receptive magick, to hold the liquids used during this kind of spell. You could use any sort of small bowl or cup for this tool. The one I use is like one of the small handle-less tea cups you see in Chinese restaurants. When I don't have my cup handy, I simply cup my left hand or both hands together.

The pentacle is the tool of the Element of Earth, the North and the physical senses. It is a flat disc with a five point star drawn on it. The surface of the earth appears to be flat but is round, and we have five senses. The pentacle is also a receptive tool. Basically, you put something on it that you want to charge or bless during your ritual. Of the four ritual tools, this is the one that I have used the least. You could draw or paint a five point star on a drink coaster or other disc of about that size but what would be even less obvious would be to use a dark colored saucer or small plate. Just pour a thin layer of salt, which is a representative of the Element Earth, in the saucer and draw a five point star in it. The salt can be poured out at the end of the ritual or simply bumped to erase the star if your ritual is interrupted. If I don't have my pentacle handy I just hold my left hand out flat, palm up with my fingers spread to represent the flat pentacle with five points.

The particular correspondences between the directions and the Elements that I have described originated in the British Isles and are traditional. Some Pagans feel that the since ours is a nature religion the correspondences between the directions and the elements should be related to the local geography. For example, Water should correspond to the East in eastern North America since that is the direction of the Atlantic Ocean or Fire should correspond to the North in the southern hemisphere since that is the direction of the equator. Whether you use the traditional correspondences as I do or local ones is your choice.

In addition to the four basic tools, you will want to have a chalice to represent the Goddess. Look for a small wine glass. You will be using this to drink juice or water during a ritual. The cauldron is also a tool of the Goddess. I have a small iron one that I bought at a hardware store. Basically, you want a flame-proof container that you can burn things in. A small clay pot would do. If you are going to be using stick incense, you will need to get or make a holder to stick it in. If you want to use cone or loose incense you will need an incense burner or thurible. You will need a sharp knife for cutting things. While a second dagger with a white handle is traditional, I just carry my pocketknife. Of course these days you have to be careful because there are places you can get in a lot of trouble for carrying a knife.

You will likely be burning candles as part of some of your rituals. Personally, I prefer to use small tapers that are about the size of your finger or small votive candles that fit inside glass holders. I occasionally use the large seven-day candles in a jar for outdoor rituals since they don't blow out as easily. You can choose the color to match the Element you want to represent or the magickal use you have in mind or you can just use white candles. Instead of buying a lot of candle holders for various sized candles try filling a bowl with sand and sticking the candles in the sand. A sand bowl will also work as a holder for incense. Never leave a candle burning unattended. Setting the woods or your house on fire would definitely not be a good thing.

It's not necessary to go out and buy all this stuff at once. You can certainly do rituals without tools just using your hands or ordinary things from around the house. Collect your tools as you need them or as they "come to you". Your altar tools should not look witchy. The pentacle and cup are nothing more than an ordinary looking cup and saucer. Your athame could pass for a letter opener, and your wand could easily hide in your pencil holder. No one is going to notice a small box of salt, a bottle of water, a cup, a saucer and an empty clay pot on one of your shelves.

Before you use a tool the first time you should to do a ritual to cleanse and dedicate it. That ritual could be very much like the one you used to cleanse and dedicate your room and your altar. I usually sprinkle the tool with salt water, pass it through the incense smoke and above a candle flame asking the Elements to cleanse and charge it with power. I then dedicate it to the service of the Goddess and the Horned God. Nothing horrible will happen if someone accidentally touches or uses one of your tools but once I've dedicated a tool for ritual use I don't use it for ordinary uses. I don't cut my steak or fix a peanut butter sandwich with my athame.

Your Magickal Name

Names are important. Your name is a part of who you are. Have you ever been in a crowd of people and someone said your name and you answered them or turned to see what they wanted and they were talking to someone else who had the same name as you? In many tribal societies a boy was given a childhood name and when he became a man he took a new name that was descriptive of who he now was. In our culture we often have nicknames we answer to as a child but which we shed when we become adults.

Many modern-day Pagans have what they call a magickal or craft name. Some have more than one. There are a couple of reasons why Pagans take a magickal name. It is a way of imitating our distant Pagan ancestors. Also, if you are not able to be open about your religion, it gives you a certain kind of anonymity. Perhaps the most important reason for taking a magickal name is that using it in ritual becomes part of getting ready for the ritual, like putting on your ritual clothes or centering before a ritual.

There is no hurry to come up with your magickal name. You may choose one that you feel is descriptive of who you are or want to be. Your name may almost choose you. When I was a kid, my name was Mike. When I became an adult, I had to sign my legal name on things so I became Michael. Much later I bought my first house and did a title search on the property. The oldest deed I could find was from the 1850's when a white man bought the property from a Native American man who had received it from the federal government in exchange for his land in the Mississippi in accordance with the Treaty of Dancing Rabbit Creek. So, my house became Dancing Rabbit Manor and some time after that I took Dancing Rabbit as my magickal name. When I think about it, the name is appropriate. I like to dance and usually walk with a sort of bouncy step. I'm shy but inquisitive like a rabbit. So, Dancing Rabbit I am.

Outdoor Sacred Places

I believe that nature is sacred. It's not a matter of making it sacred so much as recognizing that it is sacred and treating it as such. There are places that have been recognized and treated as sacred over the years and have that special feel to them. Consider yourself lucky if you can visit one of them. You aren't looking for something that special, just somewhere outdoors and private with a good feel to it.

As a Pagan, your goal is to connect with nature so it's going to be important to sometimes get out in nature to do the connecting whether it is in a park, the backyard or true wilderness. Finding places to do this is something you should begin thinking about. I grew up in a small town, have lived in an even smaller town and now live in one of the largest cities in the country. I've lived in a large house with a half-acre backyard, a tiny apartment with no yard and now a small house with a small but private backyard. Where I lived had an impact on the kind of outdoor places that were available to me and how I was able to use them. Regardless of where I lived, I was able to find safe, private, outdoor places to practice my religion. You can too if you really look and use your creativity.

One of the things you are going to be doing outdoors is sitting and observing nature. Is there a place you could sit during the day and watch the birds and other animals without being disturbed? Are there places private enough that you could do a ritual without drawing attention to yourself? Would you be allowed to light a fire in any of those places? Is there a place where you could sit outside at night to watch the moon and stars? Is there a place where you could safely sleep outside all night? Maybe this would be in the backyard, a nearby park or woods, or maybe you will have to go farther to find some place that is safe. Tell your parental person where you plan to go and about when you plan to be back. Ask permission if it's somewhere very far. It's basic courtesy and if you don't come back from a hike, they know where to start looking for you. If you go where you said you'd go and come back when you said you would come back it, will be a lot easier when you want to go on day long hikes or camp out overnight. Now, put a bookmark in this book and go walk around your backyard and over to the nearest park. When you come back, write your observations down in your Book of Shadows. What potential do these places have as a sacred outdoor place?

Another thing you will be doing outdoors is walking. Is it safe to walk around in your neighborhood during the day? What about after dark? Is there a place with trees and grass where you could walk and observe nature? Are you near enough to the mountains or the beach that you could occasionally take long walks there? How much knowledge and experience do you have in the outdoors? What things should you know before you begin taking long hikes or camping overnight? Again, more lists and more research.

What if the outdoor place you have to work with have been abused by other people who don't care about nature? What if there is litter or trash? What if it just feels unclean? You could look for another place or you could clean it up. You will need several large trash bags, gardening gloves, your pocketknife, your cauldron, charcoal, matches, a canteen of water, a sage smudge stick and a braid of sweetgrass. If you can't get the sage and sweetgrass, substitute myrrh and sandalwood incense.

Hike to the place you intend to cleanse. Put your things down in the middle of the space, center and ground yourself. As with your room, begin with the physical things. Put on your gloves and take your trash bags. Begin walking in a widdershins (counterclockwise in the northern hemisphere or clockwise in the southern hemisphere) spiral outwards from the center of your space. Pick up anything that doesn't belong there. When you fill a bag, tie it off and leave it on the ground to be picked up later.

When you either run out of trash bags or are a reasonable distance from your starting point return to the center. Look around at your work, at the bags of trash now dotting the land. Did you miss any trash? Can you see trash or litter beyond where you have cleaned? Maybe you pick it up now, or maybe you save it for another day.

Now the ritual part... Cast a wide circle and invoke the four Elements, the Goddess and the Horned God as you did in your room cleansing ritual. Carefully, light the charcoal and put it in your cauldron. Light your sage smudge stick. Again walk in a widdershins spiral outward from the center waving your smudge stick as you go. Imagine the effects of human carelessness and thoughtlessness vanishing from your sacred place. If you find an area that feels especially polluted, spend a little more time smudging it until it feels clean again.

When you have finished smudging the area, return to the center. I normally extinguish a smudge stick by rubbing it out on the earth. This may not be a wise thing to do if you there is a lot of flammable material on the ground. In that case, rub the smudge stick out on the inside surface of your cauldron. Be sure it is completely out before you either put it down or put it back in your pack. Cut off some of the sweetgrass and sprinkle it on the charcoal. As it begins to smoke, carry your cauldron in a deosil outward spiral. As you walk imagine the blessing of the Goddess and the Horned God returning to the land. If your cauldron stops smoking, stop, blow on the charcoal and cut off some more sweetgrass.

When you have again reached the boundary of your sacred place, return to the center. Extinguish the charcoal with water. Say your farewells to the Elements and the deities and open your circle as you did in your room cleaning ritual. Ground the energy you have raised and pack your things to go home. As you leave, take at least two bags of trash with you. You may choose to split this ritual into two parts. Devote one day or more, if needed, to the physical clean up and then come back and do the ritual clean up.

Remember that although the physical involves doing actual work and the ritual involves doing symbolic work they aren't two separate unrelated things. They are flip sides of the same coin of reality. Doing the physical clean up is a ritual act. The cleansing and blessing ritual that follows involves the senses and physical actions as well. They are both necessary and important.

Ritual Clothing and Jewelry

Do your need special clothing to do Pagan rituals? No, but special clothes can be fun. I have a floor length green robe and two black capes. Sometimes I wear them during a ritual and the whole process of getting dressed becomes a part of the ritual. It's a little like getting dressed up for a date or party. It gets you mentally ready and in the mood. Is it necessary? Of course not! Most of the time when I do rituals I wear regular clothes.

You might consider having a special shirt and pair of pants that you save to wear only during your rituals. They don't have to look particularly witchy. That way only you know what is special about them. You might consider making a poncho to wear during outdoor rituals. Choose a dark green or brown cloth sixty inches wide and twice as long as from your shoulders to just below your knees. Cut a T-shaped hole in the center, about six inches from side to side and about 3 inches down the front for your head to go through. Get your mother or someone who sews to show you how to hem up the ends and reinforce the neck hole so it doesn't rip out further. Put the poncho on. It should reach about from finger tip to finger tip on the sides and hang down below your knees front and back. Cut and hem it so that you are satisfied with the fit. If you want more of a cloak than a poncho, simply extend the T cut all the way down the front. You will need to hem cut edges and put a snap, button or tie closure at the neck.

You may have heard the term "skyclad" or read one of the

versions of "The Charge of the Goddess" that talks about being naked in our rites. Does this mean that Pagans worship naked? Some Pagans do and some don't. Several of the early Wiccans, some sixty years ago, were also part-time nudists who felt that nudity showed their freedom and acceptance of themselves and that it was a return to the original Paganism. No doubt our distant ancestors did some rituals in the nude but I can't imagine people in northern Europe at the close of the last ice age dancing around naked outside. They had better sense than that. Although I occasionally do a private solo ritual naked, in group rituals I've always worn clothes. I think you should use your common sense and for safety and legal reasons most of the time, wear clothes. After all, if magickal power can penetrate the walls of your house when you do a ritual inside surely it can penetrate your clothes.

The most widely recognized symbol of Pagan religion is the pentagram or five-pointed star within a circle. The pentagram is borrowed from western ceremonial magic and the commonly accepted meaning is that of the four Elements plus Spirit within the circle of birth, death and rebirth. It isn't a satanic symbol since we Pagans don't believe that a being of total evil called Satan even exists. Satan is the anti-god in Christian mythology. Anyway, Satanists usually draw their pentagram with the point down, sometimes with a goat's head superimposed on it. Pagans draw it with the point up. I have a pentagram ring and necklace that I wear sometimes during ritual. I don't usually wear them in public or at work because I don't want to put up with the hassles that would cause. Other Pagan symbols are the ankh, the triskel, the labyris and Thor's Hammer. You can find these and more in most any Pagan or New Age shop. Before you buy something like this spend some time thinking about why you want to wear it and what the consequences might be.

Another possibility as far as ritual jewelry is to make or buy a small cloth pouch to contain ritually significant objects, a Spirit Bag. I have one that my wife made that contains stones and crystals that she chose for me. I wear it on a cord around my neck sometimes inside my shirt, sometimes outside. I occasionally have people ask what's in it or what it's for. My answer is that it has some rocks and crystals in it and that it's for good luck and protection. The only time I've ever had a negative reaction from anyone was one time when I was in Oklahoma and was asked to wear it inside my shirt because it was close enough to what many of the Native Americans use that it might offend them for a white man to be wearing it openly. Do you have to have a pentagram or Spirit Bag to practice Paganism? Of course you don't. It is something you can do or not depending on your circumstance and feelings.

Chanting

I find chanting is another easy way to shift into ritual consciousness. A chant or mantra can be a word or phrase or few rhymed sentences that are repeated. Some chants are spoken like a poem while others have a tune and are sung. Unlike a song which is linear, a chant is circular like a chorus. This makes it easy to learn. As you sing or recite it the rhythm and the words of the chant give you something to fix your conscious mind on. You have chanted long enough when you feel your conscious mind become quiet and an energetic calm settle over you.

Most Pagan chants have been passed around by word of mouth so there are often several versions of the same chant and most have no known author. I've included several in this book. In my opinion, the best source of chants is a website called *Panpipe's Pagan Chants of the Month Page*. The site is especially good because it has Real Audio files of most of the chants.

Choose a chant that is calming, thoughtful or relaxing. Center and ground yourself. Begin to chant softly. As you chant, breathe deeply with the rhythm of the chant. Let the images of the words of the chant replace the constant chatter of your conscious mind. At some point you should feel your consciousness shift.

In your room cleansing ritual you raised and directed energy/power for a magickal purpose by tensing your muscles then suddenly relaxing them. Another way to raise power is through chanting. Choose a lively chant. Sing it louder and faster as power builds. When the power peaks, release it to do the work you raised it for.

Other chants celebrate our mythology by telling the story of the Goddess, the Horned God or our relationship to Them. You might choose one of these kinds of chants when you are celebrating one of the eight solar festivals, full moon or a rite of passage in your life.

I have only recently begun using the Hindu/Buddhist Om chant. Unlike a chant with English words, this one doesn't produce any mental images but is very effective in calming and stilling the conscious mind. It's great for centering. There are many versions of the chant, some quite long and complex.

The simplest version is just a simple "Om" repeated over and over. Begin by closing your eyes and taking a deep breath. The first sound is an "ah" like in "father". Slowly close your mouth and shift to an "au" sound like in "cause" and then to an "oh". As your lips close the sound should shift to an "mmm". Allow the "mmm" to continue to buzz until you are almost out of breath. Take another breath and repeat until you feel the shift in your consciousness. If stray thoughts wander through your brain or there are sounds that distract you, acknowledge them and let them go.

Flora and Fauna
For me, a big part of my Pagan path is planting and growing plants. Is there a place where you could have a small garden? If it's not practical to put plants in the ground, what about outdoor container gardening. If none of that is possible, you could grow potted plants indoors. Go to your local library and check out a few good books on gardening. Write your thoughts and plans in

your Book of Shadows.

Long before our ancestors started growing plants in their gardens they gathered plants from the wild. As a Pagan, you should be familiar with the plants that are native to your area as well as those that have been planted there. You should know the names of trees, shrubs and herbs that live near your home. You should know something about their uses. Go to your local library or bookstore and find books on plant identification. Carry one with you when you go outside. Keep a list of the ones you have identified in your Book of Shadows.

Animals are also part of nature. What wild (non-domestic) animals live in your neighborhood? Have you seen them? Do you know their names and habits? Would you recognize their footprints? Even in large cities you can spend time watching squirrels or birds. Go to the library and check out a couple of good books on local birds and wildlife. When you go for walks, pay attention to which animals you see, their behaviors and your feelings about them. Record this in your Book of Shadows.

Our ancestors kept animals, domestic animals, for food, to help with their work and for companionship. The witches were accused of having familiars, animals that they communicated with. I've had pets that seemed to know what I was thinking and who seemed to genuinely care about me. I've also had pets that were just something to feed and take care of, a lesson in responsibility but not much more. We currently have a Basenji puppy who is more than a handful and maybe just not old enough to be a familiar. However, during a ritual she gets very calm, almost asleep with her eyes open as if she is centering and grounding. So we call her a "grounding dog".

If you don't have an animal like this, consider getting one. I recommend visiting the local pound or animal shelter rather than a pet store. Ground and center yourself and reach out with your senses. Look for a reasonably healthy animal with a good personality with whom you feel a connection. Be sure you have a suitable place for your pet to live and plan for a first visit to the veterinarian. Spend time getting to know your animal companion. You may have found your familiar or at least your grounding dog.

A Circle of Friends

Everyone needs a circle of friends especially as you move into adolescence. Regardless of where you find those friends it's really important that you do find them. Some young Pagans find them in the most unlikely places. The funniest story I've heard is one a young Pagan called Nick told me.

"One Tuesday, I went to a church called Grace Christian Fellowship (GCF). This church was the "happenin" spot for all of the religious (or so-called) kids to come to youth fellowship. The girls that I hang out with at school go there, and my girlfriend goes there, so I didn't see how it could be a bad thing. So I went for a few weeks. This particular night though, I guess it was the third night, something very strange happened to me.

After winning several rounds of pool in the lounge before service, we all went down to the chapel to begin. I sang. I prayed. I almost got in trouble because my girlfriend tickled me. I laughed (under my breath) at the stereotypes and oxymorons. Everything went well. That is, until after the service when the youth pastor, Scott, pulled me to the side to talk to me. Scott: "It's good to see you here again, man. We missed you." Me: "Yea, I'm sorry I had to stop coming but the girl that was stalking me came here too. So I had to start staying home." Scott: "Oh, good reason. Listen, I was wondering if you wouldn't mind doing me a favor." Me: "Sure man, what?"

Scott: "Well, I like it when you come here because you are a good influence on some of the other guys. You are into the skateboarding, rock music, hardcore stuff like them. But you take off your beanie when you pray, and you don't sit in the back and make trouble. So, would you mind coming as often as you can to try and set some of these other kids in line?" Me: (biting hole in my tongue not to laugh) "Sure, man, I have fun when I'm here. I'll come as often as I can." Scott: "Thanks, dude!" Me: "No problem."

I thought it was weird that the only Pagan kid there was one of the best influences on the Christian kids. Well, I guess that's just the strange complexities of life. The moral of this story is: If you are a good, faithful person, you can influence anyone positively."[7]

So, should you tell your friends about your religion? That depends. Have you told your parents? They should be the first to know, and they should hear it from you directly. Assuming that is done, only you can decide whether or not to come out. I have heard from young Pagans who are open about their religion and it's no big deal. I have heard of other young Pagans who had real problems as a result of coming out of the broom closet.

What about an organized Pagan group, a coven? Most adult Pagan groups require members to be at least eighteen years old. First off, they don't want to be sued by your parents. Second, they want all the members of their group to be mature enough to understand and participate in the group's activities. Yes, I know there are immature adults too, but consider how much you really have in common with a group of adults anyway.

Your teen years are a time of great change. This puts added stresses on the already difficult job of forming or keeping a group together. There may be a successful teen coven somewhere but I've yet to run across it. Before joining or attempting to form a coven you should ask yourself why want to do this. If your main reason is to do group rituals because that's what Pagans do in the books you've read, or to be part of a clique or scene, you haven't got a good reason. If your reasons have more to do with building friendships and encouraging each other's spiritual growth, maybe you have a valid reason. Never join or form a group with people whom you wouldn't be friends with otherwise. Just because a person is a Pagan doesn't mean that they automatically have their life in order.

If you have a friend or two whom you know are Pagan, you might consider getting together with them to talk about your beliefs and do a ritual together. It would be more of a study group than a coven. You would arrive at group decisions democratically. You might just agree to follow the Rede and discuss what that means as far as actions that affect the group. There would be no oath or all-knowing, all-powerful leader. Let things develop organically and don't try to organize it into something. Leadership and structure may emerge or not. If it happens, it happens. If it doesn't, it's all good. Enjoy the time you have together and when the group ends, let it end.

Another possibility, if you still feel that being a solitary is too lonely and you need to be part of a spiritual community where you can be yourself, is to join the YRUU group at your local Unitarian Universalist Church. While YRUU is not overtly Pagan, Unitarians are welcoming to Pagan teens and UU churches are great places to grow your spirit with open minded folks. You might also look into joining a Spiral Scouts circle. They are sponsored by the Aquarian Tabernacle Church. Both groups can be found by online searches.

Now that you are beginning to understand what Pagans mean by the sacred, it's time to get more specific. Although this book is about The Horned God, we will first look at The Goddess and how She relates to us Pagan males.

Chapter 3

The Goddess: Maiden, Mother, Crone

Ancient Mother, I hear you calling.
Ancient Mother, I hear your song.
Ancient Mother, I hear your laughter.
Ancient Mother, I taste your tears.[8]

During the Upper Paleolithic, about 40,000 to 10,000 BCE, we humans were hunter-gathers living in small extended family groups. The men hunted. The women gathered plants and raised the children. Women were likely seen as the source of life since they gave birth and fed their babies with milk from their bodies. It is during this era that numerous "Venus" statues were produced. We can not prove, but it is reasonable to assume that they were representations of the ideal female, the divine female, the Goddess.

We don't know what our ancestors believed about their Goddess or what rituals they performed. All we have are artifacts, the carved Goddess figures. Even if we did know exactly how they worshiped, things have changed and we have changed. If we could copy their rituals and do them exactly as they were done, they would be nothing but copies. They found their ways to connect with the Goddess and we must find our own.

As many things in nature come in both male and female kinds, our Pagan Gods are also male and female: Gods and Goddesses. The ancient Pagans often saw their many Gods and Goddesses as distinct beings. Modern Pagans often see the many Goddesses as giving us pictures from different perspectives of the Divine Female (The Goddess), and the many Gods of the

Divine Male (The God). The Goddess and the God can be found in the cycles of the Moon and the Sun, the cycle of the seasons, and in the qualities that society calls feminine or masculine within our own lives. While it is only natural that most males will have more masculine qualities than feminine, we males do have feminine qualities. We too have the Goddess as well as the Horned God within us and to be fully whole we should connect with them both.

In your Book of Shadows, list those qualities you possess which society defines as feminine: nurturing, empathy, receptiveness and intuitiveness.

Meet The Goddess

One of the most beautiful examples of modern Pagan poetry is *The Charge of the Goddess* by Doreen Valiente. In it, the Goddess speaks directly to Her Pagan followers. I would encourage you to get a copy of *The Mother of Witchcraft* or *The Spiral Dance* and read it for yourself. In this book, however, I am using a quite different *Charge of the Goddess* by Kyri Comyn. Which version is "right"? Well, they both are. The important question is, "Which one speaks to you?" Remember, there is no such thing as Pagan 'Holy Scripture'.

I am the quickening of the seed in Springtime, the glory of ripe fields in Summer, and the peace of the quiet woods as the snow calms the Earth in Winter. I am the lilt of the maidens' melody in the morning, the patient hand of the Mother and the deep river of the mysteries taught by moonlight.

I give the creatures of the earth the gifts of song rising from the heart, the joy of autumn sunset, the cool touch of the renewing waters, and the compelling call of the drum in the dance. To you I give the joy of creation and the companion of beauty to light your days.

By the powers of the steadfast Earth and the wheeling stars

I charge thee; by the darkness of death and the white light of birth I charge thee; and by the terrible strength of your human spirits, I charge thee:

Strive always for the growth of your eternal soul, never intentionally diminish your strength, your compassion, your ties to the earth or your knowledge.

Challenge your mind, never accept complacently that which has been the standard merely for the reason that it is the standard by which the majority judges itself.

Thirdly, I charge thee, act always for the betterment of your brothers and sisters. To strengthen them is to forge the true chain of humanity, and a chain is only as strong as its weakest link.

You are my children, my brothers and sisters and my companions. You are known in great part by the company you keep, and you are strong and wise and full of the powers of life. It is yours to use them in my service, and I also am known by the company I keep.

Go forth in joy and the light of my love, turning to me without fear when the darkness threatens to overcome you, and turning also to me to share your triumphs and your achievements, and know in your heart of hearts that we are together in blood and spirit 'til the last star darkens in the sky and winter comes to the universe.[9]

Now sit down with your pencil and your Book of Shadows and record your first impressions. Over the next month and from time to time revisit *The Charge* and write down the parts that speak to you, Her Son.

The Rhythm of the Moon
All women, between puberty and menopause, experience the monthly rhythm of their menstrual cycle. This is roughly the same as the moon's 29.5 day cycle of waxing and waning. It's

only natural that the Goddess is seen in the moon's cycle. She is the one who continually changes. During waxing moon, She is the Maiden, independent and self sufficient. During full moon, She is the Mother giving birth, fruitful and nurturing. Then, during waning moon, She is the ancient Crone, death bringing, wise and mysterious. Finally, during the new moon She vanishes from the sky altogether. Astronomers use the term new moon to describe this phase of the moon when its night side is toward the earth and it is not visible. Since some Pagans use the term new moon to mean the first sliver of the waxing crescent seen a few days after the astronomical new moon, I will be using the terms dark moon and waxing crescent to avoid confusion.

Some men may feel that they can ignore this ebb and flow. After all, we don't menstruate. They believe that forging onward regardless is manliness. I disagree. We too have the Goddess within us. We can not charge forward full speed all the time. Sometime we need to stop, reevaluate, and rest. Connecting with the Goddess both within and without makes us more, not less, the men we were born to be.

One way I connect with the Goddess is to connect with the cycles of the moon. If you do not have a personal calendar or datebook, get one. Mark the dates of the first quarter, full, last quarter and dark moon in it. I use a shaded-in circle for dark moon, a reverse C-shape for waxing crescent, a D-shape for first quarter, an empty circle for full moon, a reverse D-shape for last quarter and a C-shape for waning crescent. You can find the dates for the phases of the moon in an almanac or online.

Since the moon appears to be increasing in size, the time from dark moon to full moon is a time to do rituals for increase, growth and attraction invoking the Maiden Goddess energy. Full moon is a time to do rituals that involve the full power of the Mother Goddess, a time for celebration and blessing, and for bringing projects to their fruition. As the moon seems to shrink from full moon to dark moon, this is a time to do rituals that have to do with getting rid of, weeding out or banishing invoking the power of the Crone Goddess. During the dark moon, the moon is absent from the sky. Pagans who exclusively work with the energy of the Goddess use this time to rest and refrain from doing ritual. I use it as a time for introspection, vision questing and connecting with the Horned God but more about that in the next chapter.

While you can and sometimes must do rituals involving the moon and the Goddess indoors, I believe when possible you should do Her rituals outside. When you go off to do your observations and rituals, be sure to let your parents know where you are going and about when you plan to be back. If you can't get permission to actually go somewhere at night, you could do observations from your backyard or, depending on the orientation of your house, even from an open window. Some Pagans feel that moon rituals must occur exactly at the time and date of the particular phase of the moon. I think that the day before, day of and day after are close enough.

The first quarter moon rises at noon and sets at midnight so the waxing moon can be seen best in the western sky in the early part of the night. Full moon rises at sunset and can be followed across the sky all night. The last quarter moon rises at midnight and sets at noon so the waning moon can be seen rising in the eastern sky after midnight or high in the sky during the early morning. Dark moon rises at sunrise and sets at sunset. Since you would be looking at its unlit night side in close proximity to the sun, it can't be seen.

Shortly before dark on the first six nights after dark moon, go to your outdoor sacred space where you will be away from bright lights and have a relatively unobstructed view of the sky. Look for the young waxing crescent in the western sky just after sunset. You can find the exact times and dates of moonrise and moonset each day at the *Old Farmer's Almanac* website, almanac.com/rise/. Draw the moon's approximate shape and jot down the time you saw it in your datebook. You can watch the waxing moon until it sets without having to stay up too late. A week later, if you can find a place with an unobstructed view of the eastern and western horizons, you can watch the sunset in the west and the spectacular full moon rise moments later in the east. As the moon wanes it becomes more difficult to watch at night since it rises later and later each night. If you can not go outside after midnight to watch the waning moon, look for it setting in the west during the morning hours. The moon will disappear completely from the skies for a few days at dark moon. As it waxes to a slender crescent, the cycle repeats.

Making Magick

Some rituals are for worshiping the God and the Goddess while others are designed for working magick. Magick is not something supernatural that breaks or suspends the laws of nature. It's a completely natural way to achieve results by raising power through ritual. This power or energy is the union of personal emotional energy and energy drawn from Nature. When you use magick, you change the way you experience reality. Whether or not you actually change reality directly through magick, you definitely change yourself and sometimes that's all you need. When you cleansed and blessed your room, you did magick.

To do magick you need a goal. You aren't just doing magick for the sake of doing something cool. You have some real need. Cleansing and blessing is a goal. So is manifesting a solution to a need, banishing something you don't need or looking for an answer to a question.

Magick can be done with visualization alone but usually you will be performing a symbolic act using physical things. Try to match the action to your goal. After centering and grounding, you raise energy. You can do this by chanting, drumming, dancing or tensing your muscles. As the energy peaks you will release it toward your goal. Finally, you ground any excess energy and put your things away. I usually cast a circle, invoke the elements, and the Horned God and Goddess to help me in my work, but not always.

Magick should be done when you have a need, but matching the kind of magick with the cycle of the moon is more powerful. As with physical actions, the Rede applies to magick. I believe that this means that you shouldn't do magick to harm someone and that it's generally unwise to do magick "for" someone else without their permission. If you are attacked, of course, you may defend yourself but try to limit your actions and magick to defense.

A Waxing Moon Ritual

Now that you have watched the moon as our ancestors did, through a cycle from waxing crescent to full moon to waning crescent to dark moon and back to the waxing crescent, begin connecting the Goddess inside you to the Goddess outside you through ritual. Waxing moon is a good time to start new projects and to do rituals that involve growth and increase. Assuming it is also the right time of the year, waxing moon is a good time to plant seeds. Even if it's not springtime, there are many seeds you can plant indoors and grow as a potted plant or later transplant outdoors. In this ritual you will be symbolically planting the seeds of this month's projects as you actually plant real seeds. Decide on three things that you'd like to manifest this month. You will be invoking the goddess Blodeuwedd (blow-DIE-weth). She is a Celtic maiden goddess. Picture her as a beautiful young woman with large dark eyes wearing a crown of flowers.

For this ritual you will need a white altar cloth and three acorns. Go to your outdoor sacred place before dark. Set up your altar and place the seeds on it. Wait for night. As it gets fully dark you will see the waxing moon setting in the western sky. Stand up, center and ground. When you are ready, open your eyes and walk several paces to the east. Turn to your right and begin to walk deosil in a circle about your altar. As you walk say these or similar words, "Here I cast a circle of light. Naught enter but love. Naught emerge but love." When you have circled three times and are back at the east side of your circle say, "The air that is her breath." Walk to the south and say, "The fire that is her spirit." Walk to the west and say, "The water that is her blood." Walk to the north and say, "The earth that is her body." Return to the stand before your altar facing west. Looking and gesturing upwards say, "The heights." Downwards, "The depths." Bringing your hands together, "The center." Extend your arms outward, hands open, palms outwards and imagine a line of glowing, silvery light tracing its way clockwise around your space beginning at the east until it forms a circle, say, "The circle is cast. I am between worlds."

Open your eyes and gaze for a moment at the waxing moon. Take a deep breath and begin to chant:

Blodeuwedd, fair maiden, whose flowery face
Hides mystery and magick, come now to this place.[10]

Imagine the maiden Blodeuwedd walking toward you. She is crowned with flowers. What color are they? Can you smell them as she comes closer? As you continue to chant, let your vision shift to the first of your goals or wishes. Name it. See it happening. As the power peaks, squeeze the acorn tightly and imagine the energy flowing down your arm into the seed. Place that acorn on your altar and repeat the process with the second and third acorn.

When you have finished, stand quietly a moment then say, "Maiden Blodeuwedd, thank you for your presence here. May there ever be peace between us. Elemental Powers, air, fire, water and earth, thank you for your presence here. May there ever be peace between us." Imagine the glowing circle of light fading and moving outward like a ripple on a smooth pond. "The circle is open but unbroken." Kneel or sit placing your hands on the Earth, palms down and ground. "My rite is ended. Blessed be." Quietly gather your things, return home and put them away. Be sure to plant and water the acorns when you get home. Tend them carefully as you thoughtfully work toward your goals.

Since there are twelve or thirteen waxing moons per year if you used an acorn planting ritual at each one you'd soon have a forest of young oak trees. Here are some more ideas for manifesting spells. Instead of acorns I've used a handful of wildflower seeds and scattered them to the wind at the end of the ritual. I've planted a coin at the base of a tree and tossed coins into a lake as part of wishing spells. One Spring Equinox a group that I worked with used a decorated egg. We took turns holding it and charging it with our wishes then planted it in the earth. I usually think of burning as a way to destroy something but you can think of it as a way to send a message out into the universe. Write your wish on a small paper. Hold it tightly visualizing the wish. Then drop it in a fire and as it burns imagine the energy you put into your wish rushing out to make it happen. Consider writing a rhymed couplet that summarizes your goal and repeating it as you charge the object with you wish. I'm sure you can think of other actions that you could use to symbolize the manifestation of your goals. Be creative and keep a record of your spells and their results in your Book of Shadows.

A Full Moon Ritual
One of the ways I've connected with the Goddess at full moon is through a self-blessing spell. Several authors present variations

of this spell. I'm not sure who wrote it originally. This is the one that I usually use myself. Feel free to adapt it and change it as the need and inspiration arises. You will be invoking the goddess Arianrhod. She is a Celtic mother goddess. Her name means the Silver Wheel which may refer to the Full Moon or the north circumpolar constellations that wheel round the North Star. Picture her as a beautiful strong adult woman.

For this ritual you will need a red altar cloth, your athame, a bottle of water, a small bowl, your pentacle, and some salt. Go to your outdoor sacred place before dark. Wait for moonrise. Set up your altar with the bowl of water on the west side, the pentacle with a spoonful of salt on the north, the athame on the east, and the candle on the south. Stand up, center, and ground. Create sacred space as you did before.

Pick up a pinch of salt with your right hand and drop it into the bowl of water stirring it deosil with your athame. Pick up the bowl of water with your left hand. Stand with your feet a comfortable distance apart. Gently close your eyes. Breathe deeply and slowly. Begin to chant.

Under the full moonlight we dance.
Spirits dance, we dance.
Joining hands, we dance.
Joining souls, rejoice.[11]

Visualize the stars spinning round the North Star, the full moon begins to rise in the east, and the Lady Arianrhod walks toward you. What color is her hair? What color dress is she wearing? As she stands in front of you, dip the fingers of your right hand into the salt water and touch the following parts of your body saying:

Top of head	Bless me, My Lady, for I am your child.
Forehead	Bless my mind that it may be ever sharp.
Eyes	Bless my eyes that they may see the beauty of the

	earth.
Mouth	Bless my mouth that I may speak truth with kindness.
Chest	Bless my heart that dances with your rhythm.
Genitals	Bless my penis which dances to its own rhythm.
Knees	Bless my knees that I may stand strong and proud.
Feet	Bless my feet that I may walk my chosen path.
Head	Bless me, My Lady, with your presence now and always.

Stand quietly a moment then end your ritual as you did the previous one. Say your thanks and farewells, open your circle and ground. Quietly gather your things, return home and put them away. Be careful to dispose of the salt water down the drain.

Since the full moon is the time of the peak of the Goddess's energy it's a good time to do many other sorts of magick. As you write more spells, you can use the time of the Full Moon to energize them. Create your sacred space and sit reflecting on your current needs. Narrow it down to the most pressing one and choose a spell to work toward meeting that need.

Many of the Native American tribes kept their calendar in terms of full moons. They named each of the moons of the year by the things that happened in nature that were important to them. Early settlers adopted that custom and gave the moons their own names. A little research will come up with a dozen or so sets of moon names. The ones I use are taken from those lists and roughly correspond to the conditions in southern Arkansas where I grew up. You could start with my list and change it to fit things where you live.

January	Wolf Moon
February	Snow Moon
March	Windy Moon
April	Seed Moon

May	Flower Moon
June	Honey Moon
July	Thunder Moon
August	Corn Moon
September	Harvest Moon
October	Hunter's Moon
November	Frost Moon
December	Long Night Moon

The problem that all cultures which have tried to use a lunar calendar run into is the fact that the moon's 29.5 day cycle doesn't divide evenly into the solar year. A calendar of 12 lunar months will drift 11 to 12 days a year from the solar calendar. One way to correct for this drift is to add an extra month every two to three years. I do this when a second full moon occurs in a regular calendar month. This second full moon of a month is often called a Blue Moon.

In addition to writing your full moon ritual to fit your immediate needs, you can fit the magick you do to the particular moon of the year. You might invoke the young Horned God along with the Maiden Goddess for love magick during the Seed Moon, the mature Horned God and the Mother Goddess during the Honey Moon for fertility magick, and the aging Horned God and the Crone Goddess for harvest magick on Harvest Moon. The Blue Moon is usually reserved for goal-setting magick. When doing love magick, set as a goal to make yourself more loving or more open to receiving love rather than to draw a particular person to you. You could use the Seed Moon as a time for beginning longer term projects. As a teenaged male the last thing you probably need is more sexual fertility but fertility is also productivity, wealth, increase of all kinds. As with fertility, harvest is not always literal. Those longer term goals you began at Seed Moon could be finalized at Harvest Moon. In the sample full moon Ritual you did a self-blessing spell. I have also used the time of the full moon to bless or ritually charge objects. Full moon is a good time to ritually bless a new tool or book by sprinkling it with salt and water, and passing it through incense smoke and above a flame. Another possibility is to use this time to charge a stone or crystal. You can choose a stone with a color appropriate to the kind of spell you will be doing or use one that you have found by chance. Cleanse it with the four Elements. Then hold it tightly as you make your wish or place it on your altar in the light of the full moon. Place the stone in your Spirit Bag, carry it in your pocket, or put it in a special place.

Another kind of spell I've in connection with the Mother Goddess is one called the Witch's Ladder. There are a number of variations of this spell but this is how I do it. Take pieces of red, white and black yarn about two feet long and tie them together with an overhand knot. Put a small safety pin through the knot and pin it to your pants leg. Fix firmly in your mind the goal or intent of your spell and begin to braid the strings together. With each crossing of the strings repeat your goal and see it happening. When you have only about six inches of string left, tie the strings together with square knots. Tie a small feather to each of the strings. Bless the finished charm with the Elements by sprinkling it with salt and water, passing it above a candle flame and through incense smoke while visualizing your goal. Then say, "By all the power of three times three, this is my will. So mote it be." Put your witch's ladder where you want it to do its work. Hang it over your bed or in your locker. A smaller version could go in a book as a bookmark.

There are many possibilities for full moon magick. While there is nothing wrong with using other people's spells, I've found the most effective ones are the ones I've written myself. Record them in your Book of Shadows. Expect to revise and tweak your work. Sometimes I get it right the first time. Sometimes it takes a few tries. Sometimes a particular kind of spell just doesn't seem to work for me and I try something else.

A Waning Moon Ritual

You may have found some things in your life that you would like
to get rid of or banish. Waning moon is the best time to deal with
them. You will be calling on Cerridwen who is a Celtic crone
goddess of inspiration and wisdom. Her tool is a cauldron.
Picture her as a wise loving grandmotherly woman.

For this ritual you will need a black altar cloth, your cauldron,
charcoal, matches and a few wood chips. You can buy a bag of
hickory chips at the grocery where you bought the charcoal.
After midnight go to the place you have been observing the
moon. Set up your altar. Put the charcoal in the cauldron and
light it. Sit facing east and wait for moonrise. If you can not stay
out late, you could get up a few hours before sunrise. Breathe
deeply and feel the lateness of the night.

Look at the crescent moon, stand up, center and ground. Create sacred space as you did with the other moon rituals. When you have cast the circle and are back at the center, begin to chant:

Cauldron Of Change, Blossom Of Bone
Arch Of Infinity, Hole In The Stone [12]

As you feel your consciousness shift let the image of the thing or feeling you want to get out of your life come to your mind. When it is clear, pick up one of the wood chips with your left hand and press it against your forehead. Visualize it passing into the wood then drop the wood onto the charcoal. Take a deep breath and blow on the charcoal until the wood chip catches fire. Imagine the negativity going up in smoke with the wood. If there is more than one thing you need to take care of at this time, pick up another wood chip and repeat the process. When you have dealt with everything you need to end your ritual as you did in the previous moon rituals. Pack your things and walk home.

Instead of using a wood chip, you could write the thing you wish to banish on paper and burn it. Notice that I said "thing", not person. I feel that it is usually a violation of the Rede to try to banish a person. Another symbolic act could involve charging a black stone with the thing you wish to banish then throwing it as hard as you can into the night.

I use these rituals and ones like them to connect with the Goddess by connecting with the rhythm of the moon. I don't do all three rituals each month and I wouldn't expect you to either. Some months you may only do one and another month you may do more. What if you need something and it isn't the right time of the month and you can't wait? Do the spell anyway. The Goddess understands.

The Rhythm of the Earth

Pagans also see the Earth as the body of the Goddess. The Earth is not just a dead ball of matter that we can use for our own benefit. The Earth is Holy. The Earth is our Mother. We, Her sons – Her lovers, must take care of Her. Sometimes the enormities of the problems with the global ecology are overwhelming. Each of us is only one person. What could we possibly do that would make any real difference? Personally I feel that although I can not do everything that needs to be done, I will not be overwhelmed into doing nothing. I will do those things I can do. I invite you to join me and do what you can too.

There are a number of practical things I do to show my respect for Her. I recycle. In Houston, where I live, the city picks up plastic, aluminum and iron. There are drop points at most of the schools where I recycle paper. There are private recyclers who accept glass and other metals. Every community does it differently so check with your city government and look for private recyclers. I recycle my old computers at an agency called Techs and Trainers where they salvage useable parts and build computers for the elderly and economically disadvantaged. I have recycled my old cell phones at the store where I bought my new phone. They electronically clean them and donate them to a local women's shelter. If you can't find places like that to dispose of your used electronics, check with your city solid waste department. They should have facilities to receive them rather than just pitching them in the trash to end up in the landfill. You can buy bins to separate your recyclables in or make them out of cardboard boxes lined with trash can liners. I avoid producing trash by carrying a drinking cup rather than using disposable cups and by carrying a cloth grocery bag with me to the store rather than accepting paper or plastic bags.

Picking up litter that others have thrown down is another way to honor the Goddess. Make it a practice to pick up litter as you go about your usual daily routine, going to school, the store or a friend's house. When you go on nature walks, begin by centering and grounding. Take one of those small plastic shopping bags with you and pick up litter as you go. When you are done, recycle what can be recycled and dispose of the rest. Center and ground again. Thank the Goddess that you, Her son, are able to honor Her in this way. Realize that you may not be able to pick up all the litter and next time there will be more to pick up. At least you have done something. You have done what you could.

Before humans began farming, the soil was enriched by the annual death and decay of plants. Today, this cycle has largely been disrupted by human activity. One of the things you can do to restore it is to compost. Compost is decayed vegetable matter, living dirt. Yard waste, leaves and grass clippings usually ends up in the landfill with the rest of the trash. There is no reason for this, ever.

Some gardeners use complex recipes for their compost, and turn and fiddle with their compost piles. Basically, if you just make a pile of leaves and grass clippings about three feet high in an out of sight corner of the yard and water it occasionally, it will decompose and become compost. You can add food waste like coffee grounds, vegetable tops and peelings. Keep a small bucket near the kitchen trash can to put them in rather than throwing them away. Put vegetable garbage (no meat) into your compost pile every day. Don't expect your parents to take on the additional work of kitchen scrap composting. You need to be the one emptying and washing out the bucket every day.

If you don't have a yard, you can compost in a large trash can. Fill it about half full and add a couple gallons of water. Put the lid on and secure it with an elastic cord. Park the can in an out of sight sunny spot. Check it once a week to see if it needs more water. Then lay the can on its side and roll it around to mix the compost. As you add more material to your compost, center and ground thanking the Goddess for the cycle of life, death and rebirth that you are a part of. Depending on the temperature and how much grass clippings you added, in a couple months you will have compost. It should look like dark brown crumbly dirt. If your compost consists mainly of leaves and not much green stuff, you can add nitrogen and speed up the composting process by adding your own urine to the mix. When your compost is done add it to your garden, your flower bed or just sprinkle it on your lawn.

Most of our electrical energy is produced by burning fossil fuels which adds to global warming. Anything you can do to decrease your electrical use will help. I've replaced all the incandescent light bulbs in my house with compact fluorescent bulbs because they use 66% less energy. Over the lifetime of one bulb you can save 500 pounds of coal from being burnt and save 1800 pounds of carbon dioxide from being created. The only downside to compact fluorescents is that they contain mercury. So when they do finally burn out you shouldn't just throw them in the trash. Check locally and find a place where you can recycle them. By the time this book is published other even more energy efficient bulbs may be on the market.

An even simpler way to conserve energy is just to turn things off when you aren't using them. This means not just turning off lights when you aren't in the room, but also unplugging your cell phone charger when you aren't charging your phone and shutting down your computer when are going to be asleep or when you are gone. Adjust the thermostat five degrees cooler in the winter and five degrees warmer in the summer. These things may seem small but they do have a real impact.

Besides cutting back on the use of electricity the other thing you can do to cut down on the production of greenhouse gasses is to cut back on your use of cars for transportation. I now walk or ride my bike most anywhere I go by myself inside the city. If I need to go outside the city or the weather is really bad or I have to carry lots of stuff I use a car. I do keep my car tuned up and the tires fully inflated and try to accomplish as many things as I can in one trip. Turning off the lights, riding a bike, or walking can be acts of worship of the Goddess. Briefly center and ground then focus your attention on what you are doing and why. You might quietly say, "For the Goddess," as you begin to act.

As Pagans our deeds have spiritual significance. We also use rituals to add energy to our deeds. This ritual is meant to focus your attention on those deeds you will do to honor the Goddess as Mother Earth. Go to one of your outdoor sacred places. Stand still. Center and ground yourself. Turn to the east and ask the powers of air for knowledge. Ask them to educate you as to how you should honor Mother Earth and keep Her air sweet and pure. Pause and listen for their answers. Turn to the south and ask the powers of fire how you can waste less, use less fuel, and pollute less. Pause and listen for their answers. Turn to the west and ask the powers of water how you can help keep the waters of the earth clean and unpolluted. Pause and listen for their answers. Turn to the north and ask the powers of earth to open your eyes and ears to see and hear the beauty of the earth and the things that must be done to heal and protect it. Look upward and assume the Horned God position. Ask Him to empower you as His son to protect and defend Mother Earth. Look downward and assume the Goddess position. Thank Mother Earth that you are Her son and that you will take care of Her. Thank the Elements, the Horned God and the Goddess for their help and guidance. Ground the energy you have raised and leave your sacred space. When you get home, write down your impressions, answers and plans in your Book of Shadows.

It is important as a Pagan male to connect first with The Goddess within and without. I have given you both practical and ritual ways to begin to do that. Now, let's explore our connections with The Horned God.

Chapter 4

The Horned God

Cernunnos, Horned One
Cernunnos, King of the Sun,
Herne the Hunter And Hunted
Stag God of the Earth [13]
Silver on the Tree

Meet the Horned God

As day follows night and winter follows summer so the Goddess and the Horned God are linked in the sacred dance of life. I began with the Goddess because, historically, She was first, because as men we were first dependent on our mothers, and well, you have to begin somewhere. Now let's consider the Horned God. After all, He is the title of the book though you have to slog all the way to Chapter Four to hear much about Him.

Since far back in prehistory there have been male deities who were pictured as having or wearing horns. Why horns? I believe this is because at that time men supported their families by hunting. They revered the life force in the male animals they hunted. They put on horns and animal skins in ritual to draw upon that power.

The earliest images of the Horned God are painted on the walls of caves. Since this was long before writing was invented, we don't know the myths or rituals connected with them. All we have are artifacts and our imaginations.

Go with me in your imagination back to southern France in the Pyrenees Mountains during the Upper Paleolithic Era about 14,000 BCE. The last ice age is ending and the glaciers are retreating from where they have covered Europe for thousands of years. You have just entered puberty. It is time for you to meet the Horned God and become a man.

You have left the safety and comfort of your lodge. You have left your mother and the younger children. You have fasted all day and been ritually cleansed in the sweat lodge. Your father has led you to the entrance of a cave that in later times will be called Trois Freres.

Now he lights a torch and leads you in through the dark doorway of the cave. You walk down through great halls with fantastic images of huge animals: bison, elk and deer. He leads you deeper into Mother Earth herself where it is silent except for the occasional echoing drip of water. The cavern is dark as blindness beyond the flickering of his torch.

He stops at the entrance to a passage that is not much wider than your shoulders and so low that you'll have to crawl on hands and knees. He puts a lump of grease in a small stone lamp and hugs you tightly before lighting it for you. You watch as he walks away into the darkness leaving you alone. Go back or go forward? It is your choice.

Holding the lamp with your teeth you kneel and begin to crawl. The tunnel twists and narrows. The ceiling becomes so low that you can only inch your way along on your belly. Your breath comes in ragged gasps. You taste fear but still you crawl on.

Suddenly, you emerge into a room. It doesn't feel as large as the great galleries of the animals. You hold your lamp above your head and as your eyes adjust to the darkness you see Him! Fifteen feet up the cave wall in front of you. He is both man and beast and god. He is the Horned God, the Lord of the Animals and the Lord of the Hunt. On His head is a full rack of antlers. He wears a fur cloak with a flowing horse tail. His hands are held like the paws of a bear. His penis is half erect as He dances on the wall above you. Unlike the other animals that dance around him, His large eyes stare out of the cave wall directly at you.

Then He speaks:

Listen to the words of the Horned God, the guardian of all things wild and free, the keeper of the gates of death, He whose call all must answer:

I am the fire within your heart, the yearning of your soul; the hunter of knowledge and the seeker of the Holy Quest. I, the consort and mate of She whom we adore, say this to you: You who dare to find me, know that I am the untamed wind, the fury of the storm. Call unto Me in the forest wild on hilltop bare. Look in the wild places, I am there. Look at the smallest seed that in time will push through stone, I am there. Look in your own heart, I am there. Seek me with pride and humility, but seek me best with love and strength, for this is my path, and my fury is saved for the weak and the fearful. Keep this ever full in your mind: it is better to fall upon my sword and die than to live with fear in your heart.

Hear now the words of He who is the radiance of the Sun and the taste of salt upon the tongue, He whose bones grace your every meal:

Heed my call, beloved ones. Come unto me and learn the secrets of love and sacrifice. I was born on the longest night and fated to die by the next midwinter, but I shall rise again. For mine is the grain at harvest. On swift night-wings, it is I who lay you at the Mother's feet to be reborn. I take you in, and there you learn the Mystery. Scourge and flame, blade and blood, these are mine, and gifts to you.

Every jewel has a thousand facets. Hear now the charge of They who are more than a sum of their parts:

I have been called Hermes, Odin, Mithras, Osiris, Shiva and Coyote and by many other names. You may not remember me, my children, but I remember you. I know you and I speak to you in your quest. I am the embodiment of all you are or could be. I am the choice, but you must choose.

Trickster and tyrant, scholar and warrior, vagabond and family man. My names and guises number the grains of sand on the beach and the bones in your body. You must choose, for you cannot follow all of me. Where you decide fates how you live and how you die. But until that day, my children, come dance and sing; come live and laugh, for behold: this is my worship. Hear my summons and we shall stand untouched by sword or scythe. We shall be the Oak and the Holly. We will stand tall and guard Her Earth as She sleeps.[14]

Torches are lit and the dozen or so men of your clan step out of the darkness and embrace you. You are presented with gifts, tokens of manhood, and you join them in a dance that circles round and round the cavern room. When the dance is finished, you all sit and one by one they speak to you from their experiences and from their hearts passing on their collective wisdom.

As the torches burn lower you go with the men and together you make your way through the winding passages of the cavern into a large hall. The walls are covered with thousands of hand prints. Your father puts a lump of red ochre in your mouth and puts your hand against the wall. As you chew the ochre and your saliva flows, he shows you how to spit the red pigment onto the rock wall. You spit until your hand is red from the ochre and your ears ring from the percussive sound echoing off the cavern walls. When you remove your hand, its print remains. You have made your mark on the cave wall along with all the men of your clan before you. Now you go out of the cave to make your mark in the world as a man.

No one will ever know for sure why our distant ancestors painted the walls of Trois Freres caverns. Since this was not a cave where they lived, the paintings were not for decoration or artistic expression. Most of the paintings are deep within the cave system. The paintings of animals surely were part of their religion as were the stenciled handprints and the antlered man-beast called The Sorcerer. He is about fifteen feet up the wall in a fairly small room that is accessible by either a crawlway or a larger passageway. There is a hidden ledge just above The Sorcerer where a man could have sat to be the voice of the Horned God. All this is evidence that the cave was a place where ritual was done. Other similar sites have circles of footprints in the clay floor indicating circle dances were done there.

In hunter-gatherer societies, the lives of the people depended on the success of the hunt. There were no grocery stores or fast food restaurants. These men hunted large wild animals with the equivalent of sharp rocks tied to the ends of pointy sticks. Sometimes not all the hunters returned from the hunt. I believe the Horned God represented for them the divine masculine who was both the hunted that was killed and the hunter who killed and sometimes is himself killed so that the clan may live. I adapted "The Charge of the God" by Daniel Webster Christensen into what might have been His speech to a boy who had come to the cave for his rite of passage into manhood. As you read it again, reflect on its meaning for you. Now sit down with your pencil and your Book of Shadows and record your first impressions. Over the next month and from time to time revisit "The Charge of the God" and write down the parts that speak to you, His Son.

As what men did for a living changed from hunting to herding to farming to crafts and to all the occupations that followed, the image and role of the Horned God changed. I believe He is still relevant to us today. He was and still is the most important male archetype. The Horned God exists deep within the minds of all men. It doesn't matter that we don't live by hunting or herding. He is from a time before our hierarchical, patriarchal society existed. He can teach us how to live without dominating women or on the other hand attempting to become feminine. He can become for us a pattern of what it is to be fully and truly masculine. In your Book of Shadows, list the qualities you possess which could be defined as masculine: logical, brave, a protector, a provider or someone who takes charge.

Rituals of the Horned God

There don't seem to be nearly as many rituals that involve the Horned God as there are that involve the Goddess. Some of the rituals in this section I wrote myself, others I learned over the years and have adapted. If you were the original author of any of these, please contact me and I will gladly give you credit for your work in the next edition of this book. The first ritual is a ritual bath.

Before a major ritual it is customary to prepare the space but it is as important to prepare yourself. Centering and grounding is both effective and quick. Another method is to take a ritual bath. It can also be done as a standalone ritual at the end of the day just to get rid of tension and negative feelings. You will need a box of salt, mineral oil, and patchouli essential oil. Pour four table-spoons of oil into a bowl and add four drops of patchouli. Clean your bath tub and run your bath water as hot as you can stand to hold your hand in. When the bath is full, strip off your clothing, take a deep breath, and center yourself. Touch the water with your right index finger and say, "Element of Water, Be clean for this rite." Visualize any uncleanness vanishing in the waves that spread outwards from your fingers. Pour as much salt into your cupped left palm as you can hold. Touch the salt with your right index finger and say, "Element of Earth, Be charged for this rite." Visualize a white flame of energy streaming from your fingers into the salt. Pour the salt into the water. With your right hand, stir the water clockwise until the salt is dissolved. Then, say, "Water and Earth, Blessings upon thee, as I will it, so mote it be."

Now step into the tub, lower yourself gently into the warm water. Close your eyes. Breathe deeply and slowly as you lie in the warm water. Feel all your tensions and worries and fears slip into the water and dissolve away. Feel the calm confidence flow into you.

When you are done, let the water out and watch it drain. Wash the tub. Towel yourself off then rub the oil all over your body. Remember that your body is sacred. Carry that thought with you, whether it is out to do ordinary things or to do further ritual. May you both be blessed and be a blessing. You are a child of the Horned God.

Another way to ritually cleanse yourself, called smudging, involves the other two elements, fire and air. The three herbs that I use are sage, sweetgrass and cedar. You can also smudge with incense. I use sage for banishing negative energy, sweetgrass for drawing positive energy and cedar for prayers. You can buy cedar and sage in bundles called smudge sticks. Sweetgrass is a little harder to find and comes in long braids. I make my own smudge sticks from sage that I've grown and cedar that I've harvested from a tree in my backyard. I use cotton string to tie a bundle of the herbs together, and then I let it dry for a month or so. If you can only get chopped herbs, burn them by sprinkling them over glowing charcoal.

If you are going to smudge yourself with sage, light a sage smudge stick and slowly wave it around the outline of your body. Let the smoke drift around you. Close your eyes and breathe deeply. Inhale the fragrance. Imagine your cares, worries and any negativity being blown away with the smoke. This is like taking a bath in smoke. When you smudge with cedar, let the smoke flow around you and imagine your prayers drifting up with it to the Horned God and the Goddess. With sweetgrass, you will need a fireproof container to put it in. I use my cauldron. I don't recommend that you use a sea shell because shells are related to the element of water, and fire and water don't mix. Light a block of charcoal. Place the cauldron on the floor or the ground if you are outdoors. If you are inside, be sure to protect the floor from the hot cauldron with a trivet. Cut off some of the sweetgrass braid and sprinkle it on the charcoal.

Stand above the cauldron with your legs spread. Breathe in the sweet smoke and feel yourself being energized. I use smudging not only to cleanse myself before ritual but to cleanse my ritual space and ritual tools.

Like members of other religions, Pagans pray. Before you begin praying, you need to have an image of who or what you are praying to. Who are the Goddess and the Horned God, really? Are they spiritual beings with a mind, will and emotions; sort of invisible super people? Or are they personifications of an impersonal force in us and the universe? Or maybe they are just symbols, archetypes, one way of talking about a great mystery which can not be described any other way? Are the many different Gods and Goddesses separate persons or are they different aspects of one God and one Goddess? If you ask enough Pagans you will find some who believe each of the answers is true and a few who are sure that their answer is THE answer. I don't believe there is one definite answer for a question like this. I believe that it is important for you to search for your own answers and find answers that best help you relate to the deities.

There are many kinds of prayer. The most common kind of prayer among Pagans is an invocation. You have invoked the Goddess and the Horned God when you created sacred space. You invited Them to join you within your magick circle. Now, what if you conceive of the Goddess and the God as symbols or archetypes, who are you talking to when you invoke them? One answer might be that you are calling yourself to pay attention to the divine in Nature and in yourself. The same might be said when you invoked the four Elements.

Another kind of prayer is more meditative. It is like a chant in that it is designed to be repeated until the consciousness shifts. It allows you to really get to know the deity whom you are praying to. The Rosary for the Horned God is such a prayer. When I pray it I use a string of beads so that I don't have to think so hard while I'm praying. This allows me to shift more easily into ritual consciousness.

To make your rosary you need some strong thread, eight large beads, nine small beads, and a medallion or pendant of your choosing. Cut off a couple feet of string. Begin stringing in alternation six small beads and five large beads. Slide the beads to the middle of the string. Bring the ends of the string together so that both strings will pass through the remaining beads. Then string, in alternation, three large and three small beads. Finish the rosary by tying on the medallion and trimming off the excess string.

To use the rosary you say the various lines of the prayer as you touch the corresponding bead. Ground and center as you touch the medallion. Say the chorus line as you touch the first small bead. Say the verse lines on the large beads. Continue around the circle of beads saying the repeated chorus lines on the small beads and the verse lines on the large beads. When you return to the medallion take a deep breath and begin again.

Horned One, come to me. Teach me to walk lightly upon the earth.

Horned One, come to me. Teach me the truth of both life and death.

Horned One, come to me. Teach me to truly know myself.

Horned One, come to me. I will look for you in the wild wood.

Horned One, come to me. I will look for you on the city streets.

Horned One, come to me. I will look for you in the hearts of those who love me.

Horned One, come to me. I will look for you in the hearts of strangers.

Horned One, come to me. I will look for you deep within my own heart.

Horned One, come to me. You are my Father and I am you son.

Horned One, come to me. You are the wildness within me.

Horned One, come to me and lead me back to the Mother at
    last

Could you write another prayer like this one? I don't see why not. Consider what the Horned God might look like, what He might sound like if he spoke to you or what He might teach you if you are willing to learn. Spend some time thinking about this and try putting it into verse form. It doesn't have to rhyme but rhymed couples are not too hard to write. It doesn't have to have a meter but rhythm helps. Repetition, alliteration, metaphor and simile are all poetic conventions that you can use.

The Horned God has been envisioned in many different ways. Each person who encounters Him will see Him a little differently. Some encounters happen during closed-eyed meditation, some during open-eyed observation and some during an "ah-ha moment" of realization. What might He look like? Some meet Him as a deer, a stag with seven points on each antler. Others envision Him as a deer-man who stands upright much like the drawing on the cover of this book. Still others see Him as a man with antlers growing from His head. There are paintings and sculptures of Him as a man dressed in a deerskin cloak and antlered headdress or helmet. The Horned God does not always wear antlers. Instead, He may have the horns of a bull or goat. In what forms will He appear to you? Keep an open mind and an active imagination. If you are a bit of an artist, include your sketches in your Book of Shadows.

On the night of the dark moon begin by taking a ritual bath to cleanse yourself of any negativity that might cloud your mind. Set up your altar with a brown or dark green altar cloth. In the center place a dark green candle to represent the Horned God. Center and ground yourself. In front of the candle place your cauldron. Light charcoal and when it is glowing, sprinkle cedar over it. Create your sacred space as you did in the Moon Rituals.

Light the green candle and sit before your altar with your eyes half closed gazing at the candle flame and invoke the Horned God using the Rosary for the Horned God. As you feel your consciousness shift, visualize Him walking toward you. How old does He seem to be? Does He seem to be more man or beast? What is He wearing? Continue to repeat the rosary and let your imagination have free rein. As you see His form fade into the darkness and mist from which He came, thank Him for showing Himself to you. Return to regular space, ground any excess energy, take down your altar and put your things away. Before you go to sleep for the night, record some of your impressions in your Book of Shadows.

Into the Greenwood

During earliest human times when men lived by hunting, the Horned God was the Lord of the Hunt. You can meet Him indoors as our ancestors met Him deep in caves, however, you should also expect to meet Him in the fields and forests as they did during the hunt. While we no longer need to hunt and kill animals to live and should be more concerned with learning from and protecting the animals of the forest and field rather than killing them, we still need to go out into the wild woods to meet our wild self, the Horned God.

Walking in the woods is a good way to get to know the Horned God. You might begin with simple nature walks where your purpose is mainly to observe the plants and animals, and to enjoy being in the outdoors. This is the time to invest in a Silva-style compass and some maps (or a GPS) so you don't get lost, and a small backpack to carry your things in. Choose a place not too far away where you can walk in nature without running into a lot of people. When you first enter the woods, center yourself and become aware of your surroundings. Pay attention to the sights and sounds but also to the feelings you get. Pay close attention to the trees, their shape, the color and texture of their bark, the shape, size and form of their leaves. Keep your eyes and ears open for birds and small animals. It's a good idea to bring a pocket-sized guide book to help you identify the plants and animals you see on your walk.

On your walks, if you are quiet and keep your senses alert, you may see the Horned God in nature with your open eyes. This is one such encounter as told to me by a young Pagan called Fire Eagle. "Well, I think I saw him for real kind of. Tuesday afternoon/night we got a huge snow and school was canceled. I woke up early on Wednesday and I decided to go for a walk in the woods and a saw a deer and a family. At first I saw two does and a fawn which is no big deal. I see them all the time. After a while they walked away and I went where they had been and at the top of a hill between two big trees I saw a huge buck (in this case the Horned God). I swear it was like it came out of Bambi or something. He just stood at the top of the hill and looked at me. Then I looked down. I was standing in the middle of a patch of footprints (deer footprints in the snow) that made a pentagram (without the circle but still). Do you think it was just a fluke or do you think it was Him?"[15]

What do you think? I think that Fire Eagle saw the Horned God. The Horned God is an immanent deity. He is Nature and can be seen in nature if you have your eyes open. The two opposing views of deity are transcendent and immanent deity. A transcendent god is one that exists separate and apart from the material universe in heaven or the spirit world. An immanent god is one that is here and now in you and me and everything else in the material universe. Our Pagan gods are of the immanent variety. The Horned God is not some supernatural being out there somewhere who visits us sometimes like an alien beaming in from some other planet. The Horned God is right here, right now, in everything. He is the masculine energy/principle of the universe. We encounter him when we realize that He's there. Fire Eagle encountered the Horned God just like our distant ancestors did. He felt the wonder and awe of His presence, didn't he? Sure, if he'd had a gun and shot the deer it would have bled and died. It was a real deer, not some supernatural vision. It/He was also the Horned God.

As for the pentagram of hoof prints, that is interesting too. As Pagans, we see meaning and wonder in seemingly random events. When you do fire scrying you are gazing into the randomly shifting coals and finding meaning, maybe the meaning comes from deep within your own mind. Maybe it comes from elsewhere. When you keep an interesting stone that you picked up from a place you've been it's just a stone but it has meaning for you because it reminds of the place you found it. Were they just hoof prints that happened to be in a pentagram shape? Yeah, like a beautiful sunset is just light reflecting off of condensed water vapor and dust in the atmosphere. Someone else would have just seen a big deer and some prints in the snow if they even noticed them at all but Fire Eagle saw the Horned God and His mark! With persistence and luck, you can too.

Walking in the woods is also a good way to clear your head or work out a solution to a problem. Take with you an apple, a canteen of water and pocketknife. When you get to the edge of the woods, ground and center. Ask the Horned God if He is willing to help you in this place and time. If you get a good feeling about the place, close your eyes. Breathe deeply, turning your attention inward. Form a clear idea in your mind as to what problem or question you want to find the answer. The problem may be that you just feel scattered or that you don't know what the real problem is. On the other hand, the clearer and more specific your question, the clearer and more specific the answer is likely to be. Don't have any expectation as to what the answer might be or how it will come to you.

When you know what you want to ask, invoke the Horned God saying, "Horned One, Your son calls to You. Horned One, come to me now". Open your eyes. Turn your attention to the things around you letting your gaze slowly shift from one thing to another. Listen to the sounds around you. There may be faint sounds that you ordinarily would not notice or faint smells that you wouldn't pay attention to. Repeat the question in your mind. Whisper it softly a second time. Speak it aloud a third time.

Then without thinking or analyzing, choose a direction and begin to walk slowly, steadily, silently. Allow your question to drift to the back of your mind, focus your attention outward on what you are seeing and what you feeling as your feet touch the ground. Focus on what you hear and smell as you walk along. If you see something that catches your attention, stop and examine it for a while. If you hear something above the sound of your own footsteps, stop and listen intently a few moments. Depending on the time of year there may be smells that you can identify and determine the direction from which they come. Follow your impulses. Trust that the divine masculine within you will connect with the divine masculine around you.

How long you walk depends on many things. When you have the sense that your walk is done, stop and take out your apple, water and knife. Thank the Horned God for your time with him and take a long slow drink of your water. Feel it as it runs down your throat and feel life flow back into your body. Raise the bottle in a salute and pour some of the water out upon the ground as an offering. Cut your apple in half along what would be its equator. Inside is a five point star. This is the Star of Hope. Thank the Horned God for the hope He brings you and take a bite of the apple. Savor the taste and feel energy and hope return to your body. Raise the pieces of apple up offering them to the Horned God and place them on the ground for the creatures of the woods to eat.

Take a deep breath and ground any excess energy. Walk briskly home. If you feel that you received any answers or insights, record them in your Book of Shadows. Otherwise, be sure to record as much of your experience as you feel necessary and expect the answers to come in the days ahead.

Some of your walks in the woods will be more analytical than meditative. Our ancestors had names for all the trees, scrubs, vines, and herbs they encountered. They knew which were useful to humans and which should be avoided. They were familiar with the habits of the animals they met there too. Go to your local bookstore or public library and get some pocket field guides that will help you identify the plants and animals in your area. Set a goal for yourself to be able to identify twenty species of plants and twenty species of animals that live in your area. When you successfully identify a new tree or bird or herb, make a note of it in a section of your Book of Shadows. Pay particular attention to those plants that have special uses: willow for headache, devil's walking stick for toothache and sumac or sassafras as beverages. Also, learn to identify poison ivy.

The practice of sitting out or mound sitting comes from the Norse and Germanic traditions. The king or leader would sit on a burial mound or go out into the woods and sit on a low hill to meditate and commune with the ancestors and the Gods.

Go to one of your outdoor sacred places where you can sit on the ground safely and undisturbed. If the ground is cold or damp fold your cloak and sit on it. Begin by centering and grounding yourself. Breathe slowly and deeply. Take your time. Don't rush.

With your eyes open, slowly scan the area around you within your field of vision. Pause at each thing that catches your attention to notice the details, the color, the texture and shapes of the things you see. Let your conscious mind be focused on what you see, hear and smell around you. As your consciousness begins to shift you will feel yourself become calm. Your vision will narrow as you focus intently on the thing you are observing at that moment and you will feel a detached calmness settle over you.

Now close your eyes, take a deep breath and begin to chant: "Horned One, come to me from Your eternal grove. Horned One, guardian of the secrets, reveal Yourself to me." As you continue to chant you will feel your consciousness shift again. Allow yourself to go deeper. While you are in this state or after you have returned to ordinary consciousness, expect to know or understand things that you did not before. It may come as a sudden "ah-ha moment" or just a quiet awareness but it will come.

When you feel that you have sat long enough, take a deep breath and ground the excess energy. Bring your senses back to the present time and the world around you. Pay attention to the sounds and smells. Gently open your eyes. Stretch your arms up and out then stand and stretch your legs. If you have brought your Book of Shadows with you, jot down any impressions you received.

Our ancestors walked in the wilderness a great deal. Well, back then almost everywhere they went was the wilderness. Besides walking slowly, tracking or stalking their prey, our ancestors often had to run through the woods. The act of running through the woods, dodging trees and undergrowth, not by conscious design but by reflex, is an effective way to shift into ritual consciousness and connect with the Horned God. The constant blur of things moving past and the challenge of not running into or tripping over something is quite different from running or jogging on a road or track. On a track, you can daze out and turn your attention inward to that constant stream of conscious thoughts. Here, your mind will be focused outwards and the stream of chatter in your head will become stilled.

I prefer to do this ritual in the autumn when some of the undergrowth has died back, the air is crisper and the senses are sharper. A wooded park will do but the more like actual wilderness the better. Find a place to lie down in the leaves. Take your time and get to know the place. Use the practice of mindful meditation to observe the plants and animals around you. Look closely without analyzing. Listen. Breathe in the odors of the woods. As you feel your consciousness shift, call the Horned

God and ask Him to be present in you and around you saying: "Horned Stag, come to me now. Horned Stag, live in me now. Horned Stag, run with me now."

Slowly, deliberately, rise to your feet. Reach out with your senses and imagine yourself to be a wild animal or a Stone Age hunter. Now, begin to run through the forest. You sense and avoid obstacles without conscious thought. You run without a plan. You experience the blur of forest moving past you as sight, sound, smell and feeling. Slow your pace to a jog, then to a rapid walk. When you have caught your breath, begin to run again. By repeating the cycle of running, jogging and walking rapidly you can cover a great distance without ever stopping.

When you have run enough, stop. Listen to the sound of your own breathing and your heartbeat. As your breathing slows, ease yourself to the ground. If you have brought drinking water with you, raise it in salute, drink your fill and pour the rest out as an offering. Kneel, placing your hands on the ground palm down. Thank the Horned God for showing Himself to you and ground the excess energy. You can use this ritual by itself or as part of a larger ritual. Quietly walk home and record your impressions in your Book of Shadows.

Overnight with the Horned God

Our ancestors spent time outside at night as well as during the day. Sometimes they sat outside and watched the stars or listened to the sounds of the night. Other times they kept a vigil fire and their thoughts were turned more inwards than outwards. Sometimes they were outside just for a few hours. Other times they were out all night. Sometimes the goal was to stay awake. Other times sleep or dreams were the goal. The rituals and activities in this section are intended to be done outside at night. While you can do an outdoor nighttime ritual and then return home, it is more effective if you spend the entire night outdoors.

One of your earlier tasks was to look for places you could spend time outdoors at night. I hope you have found several good places. For overnight stays, your camping equipment should be simple, almost minimalist. For sleeping you will need a ground cloth which is a sheet of plastic or waterproof cloth a little longer than you are tall and a little more than twice your shoulder width and a light sleeping bag or bedroll made of two blankets. Your poncho can double as a ground cloth. You will need a canteen, water bottle or bola to carry your water. In your pockets you should carry your pocketknife, a waterproof container of strike-anywhere matches, a small plastic bag of tinder, a small flashlight, mosquito repellant, a Silva-style compass and map of your area. (OK, maybe you take a GPS device.) Some people prefer to hang some of these things from their belt or a neck cord but personally I prefer to stuff them in my pockets. You may also want to carry a small hand axe and a folding camp shovel. If you are planning to cook your meal, bring a fork and spoon to eat it with. Consider getting a backpack that you can carry your equipment in. Cover your sleeping bag with your ground cloth and lash it to your pack and you are ready to go.

Which spot you choose depends on what you intend to do there. For stargazing, pick a place that is away from city lights with a clear view of the sky. If you intend to sit up and listen to the night, a more wooded environment would work. If you are going to do any cooking, a small clearing or at least a spot where you can see the sky between the tree limbs is best. Choose a site away from streams that might mean mosquitoes and flash floods.

Even in warm weather a fire is nice. Check the local regulations and make sure that building a fire on the ground is legal. Assuming that fires are legal, remember that you aren't building a bonfire just a small cooking or vigil fire. Choose a spot, not under a tree, toward the south or the downwind side of your sacred place and clear a three-foot circle. With your camp shovel, dig a hole one foot in diameter about six inches deep. This is your fire pit. Save the dirt so you can refill the hole before you leave.

Now go search for wood to build your fire. You are looking for dry hardwood deadfall limbs. You'll find these under an oak or other deciduous hardwood tree. Walk around looking upward until you see that type tree. Now, walk around the tree picking up any limbs that are broomstick size or smaller. Don't cut or break any limbs from living trees. This is harmful to the tree and live wood won't burn well anyway. Carry or drag them back to your fire pit.

A fire lay consists of three kinds of burnable material: tinder, kindling and fuel. The tinder is something like crumpled paper, cedar bark or clothes drier lint which catches fire easily from a match. Kindling is matchstick diameter twigs six inches to a foot long. Fuel is the broomstick-sized dead limbs. Put a fist-sized wad of tinder in the bottom of your fire pit. Break off pieces of kindling and lay them against the tinder to form a rough cone. Make another layer of slightly thicker twigs onto the cone. Next, lay two broomstick-sized limbs across the hole on either side of the cone of twigs. Lay two other limbs across the hole in the other direction. Build your crisscross of limbs three or four sticks high. Then build a flat roof of twigs on top of the crisscross. Be sure you have a good-sized pile of fuel stacked handy before you light your fire. Strike your match and quickly cup your other hand around it until the matchstick is burning. Apply the match to the upwind side of the tinder and gently blow the fire to life. Pride yourself on being able to make fire with only one match but as long as you get the fire going you are doing OK. Add fuel to the fire as it begins to burn down.

Before you leave your fire, be sure to put it dead out. Soak it in water until it is cool enough that you can put your hand on the coals. Then fill the hole with the dirt you removed from it and put the leaves or grass that you raked aside back on top.

I get shaky if I don't eat several times a day. I always carry a couple protein bars and some trail mix to nibble on when I go out in the woods. Depending on the season of the year and what I plan to do that day, breakfast is bread, cheese and fruit, or hot cereal. I don't usually cook lunch because I'm on the go and that's the hottest part of the day anyway. I eat a trail lunch consisting of a couple of sandwiches and fruit, some kind of canned meat, peanut butter or cheese and crackers. Dinner is my main meal and except for times when I arrive at my camping place after dark, it is a cooked meal.

The easiest cooked dinner is a foil pack that you prepare at home. You need a two-foot piece of heavy-duty aluminum foil, one small potato, one small onion, one sweet pepper, a stalk of celery and enough ground beef to make one hamburger patty. Wash the vegetables and cut them into bite-sized pieces. It's not necessary to peel the potato if you wash it thoroughly, but you should peel away the outer few layers of the onion. Place the vegetables in the middle of the sheet of foil in a pile about the size of your hand and not more than an inch thick. Crumble the meat over the vegetables and season with black pepper. Bring the ends of the foil up and together like a tent. Make a one-inch fold and press the fold tight. Fold again and again until you are down to the pile of meat and vegetables. Close each end the same way by making a one-inch fold, pressing it tight and folding again. Refrigerate the packet until you are ready to head out.

Build your fire and allow it to burn down to the coals. Put the packet directly onto a bed of hot coals for 20 to 30 minutes. When the food is done, you just pull it out of the fire, cut the top open and the foil becomes your plate. Remember, the food is steaming hot. You just pulled it out of the fire. Put the used foil in a plastic bag to take home and recycle. You can use foil cooking with chicken, pork or even fish but I'd start with ground beef because it's easier.

The nights of the dark moon, the three nights before and three nights after, are the best times to spend outdoors with the Horned God. If you are not an experienced camper keep it simple your first time out. Get permission. Let folks know where you are going and when you expect to return. Check the weather reports and pack your equipment: flashlight, matches, mosquito repellant, ground cloth, sleeping bag, hand axe, camp shovel, poncho, food and water. Plan to arrive at your site a couple of hours before sunset. Choose a suitable place for your fire if you plan to build one. Dig your fire pit and gather your firewood. Unroll your ground cloth and sleeping bag north of your fire near the center of your space or on the upwind side if there is a breeze. After cooking and eating your meal, you are ready to do the outdoor ritual that you came for.

If you are new to camping out alone, just sitting by your fire and sleeping out under the stars is a ritual. You will hear sounds, smell smells, and feel changes in the temperature throughout the night just as your ancient ancestors did. On your first few overnight stays plan nothing more elaborate than just success-fully spending the night out. When you have finished your meal, invoke the Horned God saying:

By leaf and branch of the great oak tree
By stag and wolf, all creatures free
Horned One, I call now to thee.
Watch over my circle through the night
'Til morning sun brings first daylight
Horned One, I call upon thy might.[16]

Then sit before your fire a while, and when you get sleepy, lie down and listen to the night until you doze off.

Besides its obvious use as a cooking fire or to keep warm, your campfire can also be used for fire scrying. If you decide to stay up a while, wait until after your fire has burnt down to coals, then sprinkle sweetgrass, cedar or sandalwood on it. Invoke the Horned God saying: "Horned One, may the mysteries be revealed to me." Sit before the fire looking into the flames. Continue to chant softly. Gaze into the coals, and let your vision soften and blur. Almost close your eyes. Breathe deeply and blink if you feel the need to. With practice you can see images or pictures in the flickering flames and glowing coals. When the coals have almost died out or you have become too sleepy, thank the Horned God and ground excess energy. Jot down a few brief notes to help you remember what you saw when you return home.

If you are camping out in the open on a clear night, you have an opportunity to get familiar with the stars. In my opinion, the best book on naked eye astronomy is *The Stars* by R. A. Rey. Read it through and study the constellations you intend to identify before you go out because it's not easy to look at a book in the dark.

If you have made camp before dark and are waiting for your fire to die down to coals so you can cook on it, you might use this quiet time as night falls to do a little star magick. Sit on the east side of your fire with your back toward the flames. While it's pleasant to stare into a fire and useful for scrying, you want your full night vision to develop as the night falls. As daylight fades and the sky turns a deep indigo look for the first star of the evening to appear. It is usually the brightest star in the eastern sky at that time of the year. It is for you the Wishing Star. Many ancient spells have been preserved for us in nursery rhymes. When you see the first star of the evening, make a wish. Visualize it. Speak it. As night grows darker and the star grows brighter say, "Star light, star bright, first star I see tonight. I wish I may. I wish I might have the wish I wish tonight." Yeah, it's silly and a little childish but that's when magick happens. Sometimes all you have to do is let go of your serious logical thinking for a moment and let your inner child come out to play.

Before you turn your attention back to your fire, turn and look at the western sky. If you see a brilliant white "star" near the western horizon, this is no star. This is the planet Venus. Since it orbits closer to the Sun than earth, it can only be seen as the Evening Star in the west after sunset or the Morning Star in the east before sunrise. Other times it can't be seen because it is passing between us and the Sun or around the far side of the Sun from us. If your wish is for love or romance, you can use the Evening Star, Venus, as your Wishing Star.

After you've eaten and cleaned up look to the north and learn to trace the circumpolar constellations. Most of the Great Bear is faint and hard to trace but it's easy to find the part that's called the Big Dipper. The Little Bear/Little Dipper is harder to see unless the night is quite clear but if you trace a line from the Pointer Stars at the end of the bowl of the Big Dipper, the next star you find will be the North Star at the end of the handle of the Little Dipper or tail of the Little Bear. Of course, real bears don't have long tails. There are a couple of myths as to why these bears have long tails. In the one I like best, the God catches the bear by the tail and throws it into the sky stretching its tail in the process.

If you continue on the line you traced from the Big Dipper through the North Star, you will come to a group of five medium-bright stars that form a loose "M" or "W" depending on the season and time of night. This is Cassiopeia the Queen. The Greek myths about her explain that Zeus put her in the sky because of her boasts about her great beauty. She is pictured as sitting upside down during the autumn when she is easiest to see as punishment for her vanity. If you can not find the Great Bear because it is too low in the sky, finding Cassiopeia will give you a rough idea of which direction is north.

Other than the circumpolar constellations, the stars rise in the east and appear to move across the sky and set in the west just like the moon and Sun. Their rising time gradually shifts each night so that you will be able to see different stars at different times of the year. As well as learning to identify the stars and constellations, learn the stories our ancestors told about them.

I have done most of my stargazing in the late summer and autumn because the weather is more likely to be favorable then and the constellations of those seasons are easier to trace. My favorite constellations in late autumn and early winter are Orion the Hunter, Canis Major the Dog and Taurus the Bull. You can find Orion in the eastern sky by looking for the three bright stars in a row that form his belt. Locate Taurus by finding the bright reddish star, Aldeberan above Orion. Below Orion is the Big Dog which contains the brightest star in the sky, Sirius. The nice thing about these constellations is that they actually look like something if you trace all their stars.

If the night is very clear, look for the Milky Way. It will look like a thin shining cloud stretched across the sky. It's actually our galaxy which is a flat spiral of billions of stars. When you look up or down out of the spiral, you see the stars which are relatively close to us and then out into intergalactic space. When you look along the plane of the spiral, you are looking at most of our half of the entire galaxy. The stars are so numerous yet far away that they look like a faint glowing streak. There are many stories about the Milky Way, that it is milk poured from the breast of the Goddess, that it is the path that the spirits of the ancestors take and that it is the starry path the God or a departed hero rides.

If you follow the Milky Way to the southwestern horizon in the summer time, you'll find one of my favorite summer constel- lations Scorpio the Scorpion. Start with the bright reddish star, Antares, and trace to the right to find his T-shaped head and pincers, then trace left and down to the stinger that curls up on the end of his tail deep in the Milky Way. Myth has it that he was sent by the Goddess to kill Orion but as a precaution the God made sure that they are never in the sky at the same time.

When you get sleepy, lie down on your sleeping bag and let your fire burn low. Look up at the stars. While you are watching the stars wheel overhead in the night sky, know that you share an experience with your distant ancestors. As you breathe in the night air and smell the smoke of your campfire, let their memories come to you as you sleep. Invoke the Horned God's presence saying: "Horned One, protect me within this circle of flickering light. Come to me from the shadows of Your holy forest. Live in my heart throughout the night." Next morning, rise and greet the new day thanking the Horned God for what you have experienced. Eat a quick breakfast. Pack up your things and be sure to leave your camp as it was before you came. Leave nothing, not even footprints. Take nothing, only memories.

Drawing in the Horned God

The last ritual in this chapter is called Drawing in the Horned God and is another way to connect with the Horned God by drawing Him into yourself and becoming the God Himself. Since this is a major ritual you should prepare by taking a ritual bath or smudging and putting on your special clothes beforehand. Go to your outdoor ritual site before dark and set up your altar with a green cloth toward the north side of your space. Place a token of the Horned God in the center of your altar. You might use a phallic symbol such as a thyrsus, which is a wand with a pine cone at the tip. I have a rack of deer antlers that I use for this purpose or you could use your athame. Dig your fire pit toward the south side of your space, build your fire lay, and gather enough extra wood to last the night. After a light meal, sit before your fire. Center and ground yourself.

When you are ready, cast your circle either by visualizing the circle forming to surround your space or by walking deosil in a circle around your space. Once the circle is cast, walk to the east side of your space and say, "Spirit of Air, blow into this time and space. As I breathe in let me become one with the Horned God and know His life in me." Walk to the south side of your space, and say, "Spirit of Fire, ignite this time and space. As my determination is kindled, let me become one with the Horned God and feel His will blazing in me." Walk to the west side of your space and say, "Spirit of Water, flow into this time and space. As my emotions are steadied, let me become one with the Horned God and feel His compassion in me." Walk to the north side of your space and say, "Spirit of Earth, ground this time and space. As I become rooted here, let me be confident and become one with the

Horned God for His seed is within me." Turn to your right walking past your altar to stand before your fire for a moment. Turn again to your right to face your altar. Fold your arms in the sign of the Horned God and say: "Horned God! Hail and well met. Bless this time and space, and bless me for I am your son who stands within the sacred circle calling your name."

Sit down facing your altar, close your eyes and breathe deeply. Chant the names of the Horned God or repeat the Rosary of the Horned God until you feel yourself shift into ritual consciousness. Visualize yourself sitting before your altar and from the darkness on the other side of the altar you see a radiant light the color of leaves in the springtime. Out of this light steps the Horned God. His face is in shadow as He walks toward you. He holds out to you a leather pouch on a cord as a gift. You reach out and take it. As you accept the gift, you see yourself reaching upwards. You blink and you realize that you are seeing yourself through His eyes. You see yourself as you take the pouch and hang it around your neck. As the pouch touches your chest, your body changes, matures, grows strong and masculine and from your head spiky antlers begin to grow. Your vision shifts again and your newly maturing self watches as the Horned God turns, and with a wave of His hand walks back into the radiant green light of the forest and is gone. Your antlers grow and branch. You feel the Horned God's power surge through your body, and you know that He has not gone but is in you and you are becoming Him. Take a deep breath and gently open your eyes. Sit quietly for a while and savor the experience. When you are ready, stand and thank the Horned God for showing Himself. Thank the Spirits of the Elements for their help with tonight. Close your eyes and imagine the circle expanding and growing fainter until it disappears into the night. Kneel placing your hands on the ground palms down and ground any excess energy.

The Drawing in the Horned God ritual can be a ritual unto itself, a way of worshiping the Horned God. It can be used as part of a larger ritual to raise power which you can then direct into an object or to accomplish a specific goal. It could also be a part of a ritual in which you dedicate yourself to the service of the Horned God.

Dedication and Initiation

Dedication and initiation are two distinct events. In some covens a dedication ritual is part of the process of joining the coven. Potential new members are dedicated to study for a year and a day. The year and a day gives the candidate time to learn about the coven and their practices and coven members time to learn about the prospective new member. At the end of the time, if both are agreeable, the candidate goes through an initiation ritual and becomes a full member of the coven.

Because I came into Paganism as a solitary without a coven to belong to, because my path is non-hierarchical, non-authoritarian and not part of an established tradition, I view dedication and initiation differently. Once you have learned enough of the basics to determine that this is the sort of spiritual path you intend to follow, you may decide to dedicate yourself to the Horned God, Goddess and Their path as you understand it. After you have been walking the Pagan path for some time, when the time is right, you will have a peak experience in which the Horned God and the Goddess initiate you. I have more about that in the final chapter. So, in my experience Dedication is something that you do while Initiation is something that the gods do for you or to you.

You can use the Drawing in the Horned God ritual as part of your dedication ritual. After you have created sacred space and Drawn in the Horned God, say: "I dedicate myself now to your service, O Horned God, and to the service of the Goddess whom you adore. I shall henceforth be known to you as _____ (give your magickal name). I promise and swear to live my life by the Rede: "An' it harm none, do as ye will" and to walk gently and courageously on the earth. The hand of the Goddess is upon me. The path of the Horned God is before me. All this I swear by my sacred honor."

Having done the ritual work you came for, unless you plan to keep a vigil all night, allow your fire to die down to coals. When you have said good night to the Horned God crawl in your sleeping bag and get some sleep. In the morning, sit up, look around and greet the new day. After you have eaten a light breakfast, pack up your things and erase all traces of your fire. Before you leave your space, walk a spiral path widdershins beginning at your sleeping place. Pick up any litter you find and as much as possible return the site to the conditions it was in before you came. When you get back home, put your things away, get cleaned up, and briefly record your experience in your Book of Shadows.

Horned Magick

I don't believe that there is a particular kind of magick that belongs exclusively to the Horned God or to the Goddess. Some call projective magick masculine and receptive magick feminine but often magick is both projective and receptive or neither. I usually invoke both the Horned God and the Goddess during ritual asking for both Their help. However, since the physical protection of the family and the tribe has traditionally been the job of the men, I am including examples of those kind of spells here.

There are times when you are in places and situations where you need personal protection. While magick spells don't take the place of staying alert and using good sense, they can be useful in augmenting your physical senses and your logical mind. In addition to physical and verbal assaults there is the whole area of psychic assaults and picking up negative energy from people and places. I am not one of those paranoid folks who believe that there are people out there just waiting to cast an evil spell on me.

Fighting things that don't exist is like worrying about things that haven't and aren't likely to happen. It just creates fear and negative energy that doesn't need to even be there. However, since I am an empath, there have been times and situations I've found myself inside someone else's head feeling their emotions as they were feeling them. It's a bit like John Coffey in the movie *The Green Mile*, except that I've never brought a mouse back to life or made light bulbs explode. While empathy can be useful, there are times when I don't need to be sucked into someone's black hole of neediness, or have my emotions manipulated by someone else to my own detriment. For these times and when I know I'm going to be somewhere that is more dangerous than usual, I use a personal shielding spell. The year I worked at an alternative high school, I did this every morning before I went to work and none of my gangster students even tried to lay a hand on me all year, I didn't come home each day drained by all the negativity in that place and the principal was really nice to me too.

There are many different shielding spells but they can be sorted into three main categories by what they do with incoming energy. They can scatter, absorb or reflect it. In creating a reflective shield you visualize yourself surrounded by a silvery bubble or wearing shiny armor. You can hold a piece of hematite or a small mirror while you do the spell to help you visualize. The reason why I don't usually use this kind of shield often is that by reflecting the incoming energy back to its source people often perceive it as you sending negative energy to them. An absorptive shield involves visualizing yourself surrounded by a thick wall or dark cloud. The energy that hits it is absorbed and grounded. The problems I have with this kind of shield are that it leaves me psychically blind and takes energy to maintain. When I shield, I usually use a scattering shield. This allows me to protect myself without completely shutting off all incoming energy and without antagonizing people around me. People who are better at visualization than I am use the image of being surrounded by white light. I've never been too successful with just visualizing a shield so I use incense smoke to help me. When should you shield? I have talked with Pagans who shield on a daily basis or shield mainly during ritual. I only shield when I have a serious need. Experiment with different kinds of shielding and see what works best for you. The following is the spell I typically use for shielding.

Go to one of your sacred places where you can be alone and undisturbed. Light a stick of incense, center and ground, invoke the four Elements and the Horned God. Holding the incense high in your right hand begin to turn deosil. Say, "About me I cast a web of light. Naught enter but love, naught emerge but love." As you turn, slowly lower your arm and allow the smoke to wrap around you. When you are wrapped from head to foot in a spiral of smoke continue turning but now wave the incense slowly up and down. Imagine the trail of smoke weaving a magickal cocoon around you. Thank the Horned God and the Elements for their help and ground any excess energy. You will be able to see through the shield and empathically feel through it so you will know what's going on around you. Negative energy not penetrate it. At the end of the day or when you no longer need it, simply close your eyes and imagine the cocoon splitting on one side, unraveling, and vanishing as it falls away from you.

There are times when you will want to magickally protect a place. This is called setting wards. I do it around my house when I go away for a few days. I've set wards around my car before a particularly stressful trip and one time around my campsite. Stand before your house, center and ground. Quietly invoke the Horned God. Holding your wand in your right hand, walk around the outside of the area deosil. As you walk say, "Here I cast a circle of protection. Naught enter but love. Naught emerge but love." Stop at each of the four directions to invoke the help of the Elements. Stop at the windows and doors. Examine them carefully. Are they locked? Are they secure? If you are setting wards around your car, are the tires good and properly inflated. Does it have the proper level of oil and other fluids? With your wand trace a pentagram in the air over the doors, windows, tires or whatever. When you have finished casting your circle, thank the Horned God and the Elements. Ground any excess energy. Secure any doors or windows that were not secure. Top off the fluids that were low and take care of any tire problems. Don't worry about breaking the circle when you step through it. This circle was not designed to keep you or anyone else who is friendly out. When you return from the trip or get ready to sell the car, remove the wards in much the same way you open a circle at the end of a ritual.

I have given you two examples of protective spells. Use them as you need them. Adapt or modify them as it suits your needs and be ready to create new spells. Don't let protective magick become an excuse to become either paranoid about psychic attacks or complacent about taking care of physically securing things.

The Horned God in the City

When I lived in a small rural town going out into the woods or fields to hike or camp out was easy. Now that I live in a large city it's a lot harder. I have to drive a couple hours to get to out into the countryside. I can't just pick any old field or woods to go walk or camp in because I don't know the owners. There are things I can't do in a state park either because of park rules or the presence of other people. Can you really find the Horned God without going into the wilderness? It's not as easy but yes, you can. Do you remember the Charge of the Horned God at the beginning of this chapter? In an earlier version of the charge, the Horned God said, "Call unto me in the forest wild and on hilltop bare and seek me in the darkness, bright. Look in the wild places, I am there. Look at the smallest seed pushing up concrete, I am there. Look into your heart, I am there."[17] While the Horned God is found in nature, nature is not just in the wilderness. Nature is also in the city and inside you and inside other people. Connecting with nature is more difficult in the city, but it's not impossible.

The outdoor rituals I've described could be done in a city park or your backyard. If you live in an apartment with no private green space, the rituals could be moved indoors with some changes, like using a candle for your campfire or cooking your camp meal in the oven. Bring some plants or greenery inside. Bring your memories of walks in nature with you. If you can not camp out at night, you could try sleeping on some blankets on the floor with a window open.

Since I live in a large city and can't walk in the wilderness without having to drive considerable way to get there, I connect with nature by spending time lying on the picnic table in my backyard, looking up through the limbs of a huge live oak tree that practically covers the whole yard. Watching the squirrels and blue jays, and feeling the sense of three dimensional spaces among the twisted limbs is almost as good as being out in the woods. I take my walks along the quiet streets and with our Basenji in one of the dog parks.

I spend more time gardening now, connecting with the Horned God as Lord of the Harvest rather than as Lord of the Hunt. I have the opportunity to share ritual and discussion with other Pagans. Also, being away from the forest and fields most of the time makes times that I do get to go outside the city more special. So there are advantages and disadvantages to wherever you happen to live, but regardless of where you live you can find the Horned God if you look for Him.

Chapter 5

The Horned God and the Goddess

Horned One, Lover, Son,
Leaper in the Corn.
Deep in the Mother,
Die and be reborn.[18]
Buffalo

The Changing Faces of the Goddess and the God

The beginning of the Neolithic Period, about 10,000 BCE, was marked by the discovery of agriculture. Humans learned to grow plants for food rather than gathering them wild. They learned to raise domestic animals rather than hunting wild ones. Our ancestors were able to live in larger settled groups that eventually became cities rather than in small extended families that moved from place to place following the herds of wild animals. This drastic change in how humans made their living changed the way they saw the Goddess and the God. Since food now came from planting, growing and harvesting crops, the Goddess was seen in the Earth Herself. The God was seen in the Sun that warms the Earth, seed that was planted into the Earth and the grain that is cut down and harvested. The God's energy was also seen in the strength and sexual prowess of newly domesticated animals such as the goat and the bull. These changes didn't happen everywhere at the same time. They didn't happen in a single generation. In most societies, hunting and gathering continued to supplement agriculture.

Two of the earliest Neolithic civilizations that began around 7,000 BCE were in Mehrgarh, Pakistan and Çatalhöyük, Turkey. Both civilizations built what were really more like large villages than cities. The adobe buildings were multipurpose, serving as homes, temples, workshops and shops. There is no evidence of any sort of central government or military. These civilizations raised various grains and livestock outside the city which was neither walled nor protected. The predominance of Goddess statues suggests that their religion mainly worshiped the Goddess. However, there were also murals of bulls in the same rooms with the Goddess statues.

The centers at Harappa and Mohenjo-Daro that succeeded Mehrgarh during the Bronze Age, in addition to Goddess statues, produced relief carvings of a horned god who is seated in a yoga position surrounded by animals. We know very little about this god because the writing that was used by this civilization has not been decoded. Some identify this horned god with the later Hindu deity, Pashupati, whose name translates "Lord of the Animal". Bronze Age civilizations like the Minoan civilization in Crete produced goddess statues as well some paintings and small statues of horned male gods. Both civilizations seemed to have worshiped both a mother goddess and a horned god, and both seemed to have been rather peaceful egalitarian societies.

During the Iron Age there was a major shift in people's view of religion and relationships between men and women. People from the deserts of the Middle East who were shepherds and people from the plains of central Asia who were part of a horse-riding culture invaded and conquered the farming culture. In their religions the Goddess was either subservient to male warrior sky-gods, who demanded animal sacrifice or were totally absent. There was also a shift toward a more hierarchal and patri-archal culture in which women were subservient to men, and most men were subservient to the rulers. This rule by men or at least the men at the top of the social structure is called patriarchy. It has been almost as detrimental to men as it has been to women.

The Iron Age Celts in northwestern Europe did, however, worship a horned god. His image is on a silver vessel about 30 inches in diameter and about 16 inches high, crafted around 150 BCE which was discovered in a peat bog near Gundestrup, Denmark. It is called the Gundestrup Cauldron. One of the interior panels shows a man with antlers wearing Celtic pants, tunic and belt, seated cross-legged holding a torc in one hand and a horned snake in the other. He is surrounded by animals: a deer, a wolf, a lion, ibexes and a fish. There are some 60 other carvings depicting an antlered deity from this period. One which was found in Paris during the excavation of Notre Dame Cathedral bears the inscription "[_]ernunnos", the first letter having been obliterated. From this we know that His Latinized name was probably Cernunnos which would mean "Horned One". We don't know what His name was in the native Celtic language.

We also don't know the meaning of objects that are associated with Him. The antlers could symbolize His sexual prowess or could just denote Him as a hunter. The torc is a symbol of royalty or authority. The snake could symbolize healing, death and rebirth or perhaps wisdom. He sits cross-legged, which may be a meditative position or simply how a Celtic hunter would sit. The animals which surround Him may just mean that He is Lord of the Animals and the leader of the hunt. On the other hand, it could also mean that He conducts the souls of the dead to the next world. We don't know for sure what these symbols meant to the people who crafted the Gundestrup Cauldron, but we can ask, "What do they mean for us"?

The religions of Classical Civilizations of Greece and Rome and the Norse culture of far northern Europe were a blend of the religion of the Goddess and the newer religions of the male sky-gods and their subservient goddesses. There are layers or generations of gods in the pantheons of these cultures. In the Greek pantheon there are the elder Titans and the younger Olympian gods, and even generations of gods before the Titans. In Norse mythology there were the Vanir who were earlier earth deities, and the Aesir who were warrior sky deities.

Although the dominant gods were usually not envisioned as having or wearing horns, the horned gods did not totally vanish. There was the Greek Pan and Dionysus, and the Roman Faunus, Sylvanus, Bacchus and Liber Pater. We not only have artifacts but we can read the literature written about them. The statues of Pan show him as a rather small bearded man with the legs and horns of a goat. His name has been translated as either All or Herdsman. He was the patron of shepherds and woodland creatures. There are numerous stories about Pan's adventures, but we know little about the details of the rituals of his worship since rituals were often secret.

Modern Paganism attempts to return to the earlier more-balanced view of the Goddess and the Horned God, and the ideal of an egalitarian relationship between men and women. We see the Goddess in the cycle of the moon and the seasonal greening of the earth. We see the Horned God in the Sun which provides light and heat to the earth and all living things on it and which goes through the annual cycle of the seasons. We also see Him as the seeds planted into the Earth in the spring and the harvesting in the fall. We worship Him as Horned God because, although we no longer hunt for our living, we still have a need to connect with the wild and free. In this chapter, you will learn to connect with the Horned God in His dance with the Great Goddess in myth, ritual and practical actions.

The Wheel of the Year

The Wheel of the Year is the Pagan calendar of eight seasonal festivals: three planting festivals, three harvest festivals and two solstice festivals, borrowed and adapted from the festivals of the ancient British Isles. In ancient Celtic Britain, the year was divided into light and dark halves. The dark half began around November first, with the festival of Samhain (sau-wain or sah-vain) which marked the end of summer when the harvest was finished and the excess livestock was killed in preparation for the coming months of winter. Oddly enough this was the beginning of their new year. Samhain also was a time to honor the ancestors and the recently departed. The light half began around May first with the festival of Beltane, which celebrated the beginning of summer when all danger of frost has past, the hawthorn blossoms and the cattle were driven back into the pastures. Beltane was a time to celebrate fertility and sexuality.

The other two Celtic festivals were related to herding and farming. Imbolc around the first of February celebrated the birth of the lambs and promise that spring would come as the snowdrop flowers pushed their way up through the snow. It was dedicated to the goddess Brigid who is the patron of the forge and flame, music, poetry and the healing arts. Lughnasad or Lammas was celebrated around the first of August. Originally, it was a festival of games and competitions in honor of the god Lugh's foster mother, Tailtiu. Lugh or Lleu was the Celtic god of many skills. The second meaning of this festival is found in its other name, Lammas or loaf mass. It was a celebration of the beginning of the wheat harvest.

The megalithic sites such as Stonehenge have stones aligned to the rising of the Sun on the solstices, so it is reasonable to assume that they had some kind of ritual celebration at that time. Much later when the Anglo-Saxon tribes invaded Britain they brought with them their own solar festivals which were celebrated at the solstices and equinoxes. The most important of which was Yule at Winter Solstice. Solstice means "sun stands still". On Winter Solstice the Sun stops its apparent daily movement south, appears to stand still for a few days, then begins to move back northward. The Sun is reborn and the days get longer. Summer Solstice is just the opposite. The Sun stops moving northward and the days begin to be shorter.

Equinox means "equal night". It is a time when day and night are equal in length. At Spring Equinox the light is over taking the darkness while at Fall Equinox darkness overtakes light. Both are a time of balance. There is evidence that the Anglo-Saxons celebrated Winter Solstice, Yule, as the birth of the new sun and Spring Equinox, Ostara, as a spring fertility/planting festival. Less is known about how they celebrated Summer Solstice, Litha. Fall Equinox, Mabon, is now celebrated as the second harvest, the apple harvest and the second time when light and dark are in balance. However, there is little evidence that it was celebrated in ancient times or that the name, Mabon, has ancient roots.

The Wheel of the Year is more than just a cycle of ancient seasonal festivals. It is the central myth of modern Paganism. Remember, a myth is a story that teaches a sacred truth. There are today several myth cycles in use by Neopagans because our current mythology is based on interpretations of several ancient mythologies. The one that I find the most meaningful traces the life of the Horned God and his relationship to the Goddess.

The Horned God is born on Yule, the night of the Winter Solstice, and His birth is celebrated with gifts as light emerges from darkness. The Goddess having given birth in the Otherworld goes to sleep. Evergreens, mistletoe, holly and blazing fire are echoed in the colors of red and green associated with this festival. You can participate in most of the secular Christmas activities: caroling, giving gifts, wassailing, and decorating an evergreen tree remembering their Pagan origins. Even if you have to attend Christmas Eve candle lighting or midnight Mass with your parents, let the words flow over you and enjoy the symbolism of the rebirth of light in the midst of darkness.

At Imbolc, the Goddess recovers from childbirth, awakens and once again becomes the Maiden. The Horned God is still a young boy who has been fed milk from the sacred cow as the Goddess slept. He is becoming stronger and the first promise of spring can often be seen although the weather is usually at its coldest. This is a time when you should do your early spring cleaning, cleanse and purify yourself, and work on any healing you need to. It is also a time to celebrate with music, poetry, and storytelling.

At Ostara or Spring Equinox, light and dark are in balance, the Horned God begins his courtship of the Goddess and the earth awakens. It is a time for planting when the seed of the Horned God is planted into the body of the Goddess as physical seeds are planted into the earth. Some traditions celebrate the union of the Horned God and the Goddess at Beltane but if you count back nine months from the birth of the Horned God at Yule you arrive at Spring Equinox so it makes sense to me to celebrate this festival as their first sexual union rather than Beltane. Ostara is named for the Germanic goddess of dawn and spring whose familiar is the rabbit. You can celebrate it by planting seeds, inside in pots if it's before the last frost of the year where you live and by coloring eggs, and well, by many of the other "Easter" customs of our culture. While Christians celebrate the resurrection of their savior, you can be celebrating the resurrection of Nature.

By Beltane the earth has fully greened and flowers are in bloom. Phallic maypoles were thrust into the earth and the people danced around them weaving colorful ribbons round the pole. Cattle were driven between smoking bonfires to purify them before they were taken to their summer pastures. Couples went into the woods to collect flowers and spent the night together re-enacting the sexual union of the Horned God and the Goddess. The movie, *The Mists of Avalon*, does a good job of portraying what the ancient Beltane festival might have been like. While you might not be old enough (even in ancient times) to fully participate in the Beltane festivities, you can celebrate the greening of the earth, the flowering of projects you have started earlier, and, yes, your budding sexuality.

Litha or Summer Solstice marks the peak of the Horned God's strength as the Sun's energy is poured into the Earth's plants. He is enthroned as the Lord of the Greenwood with his Queen, the Lady of the Forests. In agricultural societies the crops were established, laid by, and harvest was weeks away so there was a pause in the work, a time to rest. This is a time when the veil between the worlds is thin and all sorts of light-hearted magick is possible. Think of *A Midsummer Night's Dream*. One way you could celebrate Litha would be to spend the day at the beach or picnicking in the park with your friends or family.

At Lughnasad or Lammas the grain is harvested and baked into bread. The grain must die so that the tribe may live. The Horned God has sowed his seed into Mother Earth and poured his energy into the crops, then offers Himself as a sacrifice. There are parallels here to Christianity but there are important differences. This is not a sacrifice in payment for sin to pacify an angry deity. This is a willing and useful sacrifice to feed the people. You could bake bread and eat it around your campfire, offering toasts to your accomplishment. Yes, you can actually bake bread. Our ancestors did it. I do it. You can learn how to do it. Try making a loaf in the rough shape of a man to represent the God. If you aren't quite ready to try your hand at baking you could craft small figures out of wheat or corn husks, charge them with power and save them until the next planting season.

On the Mabon or Fall Equinox, light and dark are once again in balance. The Goddess becomes the Crone and the Horned God prepares to cross over into the Otherworld. Mabon is the second harvest or the apple harvest in many parts of the world, which occurs after the grain harvest. When I lived in the Mississippi Delta country the cotton harvest was in progress and farm workers took advantage of the Harvest Moon to work into the night. It is a time when light and dark are in balance so magick that celebrates or promotes balance fits in here. Most places this is when the first coolness of the coming winter is felt so it can be a very pleasant time to be out in the woods or fields.

By Samhain, the Goddess prepares to follow the Horned God

into the Otherworld. She doesn't die but She does change. The veil between the worlds is again thin and the spirits or at least the memories of our ancestors can visit the land of the living. Spend time naming, remembering and honoring your ancestors and beloved dead. If your family celebrates The Day of the Dead, celebrate with them. If your friends are going to a Halloween party, go with them and have fun. You are likely the only one there who knows the origin of most Halloween customs.

We don't know the details of how our ancestors celebrated the eight festivals or if they even celebrated all eight. We aren't farmers and herdsmen as they were and so we wouldn't actually be celebrating the wheat harvest or the lambing season anyway. Furthermore, most of us live in parts of the world where the seasons start and end at quite different times of the year than they do in Britain, where the myths originated. How then are we to celebrate the life, death, and rebirth of the God in a way that is meaningful to us today? That is the challenge. In the next section I'd like to look at the typical format of a Pagan solar ritual, an example of a Samhain ritual, and some ideas that will help you write your own rituals.

A Sample Samhain Ritual

By now you have conducted quite a few Pagan rituals. I'd like to quickly look at the basic pattern you followed so that in this section you can begin creating your own. A ritual should have a purpose, a reason why you are doing it more than just because you are a Pagan and that's what Pagans do. The rituals you have done so far largely fall into the category of magickal workings. The eight solar festivals or sabbats are as much about celebrating the myth of the Wheel of the Year as doing magick. A sabbat ritual is like a three-act play. In the first act you are preparing yourself and the space where you will do the ritual, inviting the Elements and the Gods and casting a circle around your space. The second act of your ritual includes a re-enactment of the myth of the Wheel of the Year, a celebration and acts of magick. In the third act you say your farewells to the Gods and the Elements, release the circle and ground energy you have raised. I have written the Samhain ritual for you in some detail. You may choose to use it exactly as written or modify it. My intention is that you will use the pattern of the Samhain ritual to write the other sabbat rituals yourself.

The Samhain Ritual was written as an outdoors nighttime ritual. If you are unable to do an outdoors ritual, don't despair. You can still do the basic ritual indoors and that gives you time to go to a Halloween party with your friends or pass out candy to young trick-or-treaters at your door.

The purposes of the ritual are to honor the Horned God as Lord of the Dead and the Goddess in Her Crone aspect, remember your ancestors, your loved ones who have died and celebrate the harvest of your accomplishments this past year. Build a small fire near the center of your outdoor sacred space and set up your altar near the north side. Cover your altar with a black cloth. Place a plate with an apple and a pomegranate on it near the center, and a chalice of apple juice. Put a black candle on the left side, an orange candle on the right, and a white candle between them. Put pictures or tokens of your ancestors on the altar as well.

Sit with your back to your fire, center and ground. When the fire has burned down to coals, stand down wind of the fire and sprinkle a handful of sage on it. As the sage smoke swirls around you, imagine the cares of your day being carried away with the smoke. Walk to the east side of your space and begin walking in a deosil circle around the central fire. Visualize a glowing circle forming where your feet touch the ground. Walk around your circle faster the second time around and still faster the third time. Return to the center and facing east say, "Night breezes, you who blow the autumn leaves about. I call upon you for my rite. Come to me now, on this Samhain night." Face south and say, "Blazing fires, you who warm me through the autumn chill. I call upon you for my rite. Come to me now, on this Samhain night." Face west and say, "Flowing streams, you who quench my thirst and stir my soul. I call upon you for my rite. Come to me now, on this Samhain night." Face north and say, "Fertile soil, you who support my feet as I walk the earth. I call upon you for my rite. Come to me now, on this Samhain night." Walk to your altar and light the black candle saying, "Ancient Mother, keeper of the cauldron of rebirth, Lady of Light and Shadows. I call upon you for my rite. Come to me now, on this Samhain night." Light the orange candle saying, "Horned One, leader of the wild hunt, Lord of Light and Shadows. I call upon you for my rite. Come to me now, on this Samhain night." Light the white candle saying, "Fathers of my father and mothers of my mother, my ancestors bright. I call upon you for my rite. Come to me now, on this Samhain night." Walk back to your fire and stand facing north. Bring your hands together in a namaste gesture then stretch your arms outwards palms out and say, "My circle is cast. I am between the worlds."

Sit quietly by your fire, close your eyes and breathe deeply. In your imagination you begin to hear the rapid hoof beats. A running deer is approaching. Now you see Him, the Horned God in the form of a stag who runs on two legs is racing toward you. He nods His antlered head and reaches down with a strong hand lifting you up onto His back. You hold on tightly as He runs through the forest. Ahead in the moonlight is a clearing and tall hill. As you race closer toward the hill you notice a pair of standing stones that frame a dark opening like a doorway into nothing. Without slowing, He gallops between the stones and down into darkness. Knowing your fear the Horned God says, "Don't be afraid. All who live must pass this gate." He takes you deeper until you arrive at a great sunlit field of flowers. Birds sing and butterflies flit from flower to flower. You see children playing among the flowers and older people resting beneath the trees. The Horned God whispers to you, "This is Summerland, the place where the departed rest and enjoy their reward." You want to join them but the Horned God runs on. As you move into a shady valley, fog and mist roll in. The trees are a blur of gray shadows. Ahead you see a golden light. You see a shadowy figure moving through the fog toward the light beyond. "This," says the Horned God, "is one who has rested and is returning now to the land of the living." You have no chance to try to follow the figure because the Horned God turns and runs back into the forest. You emerge from the forest once again but this time there are no flowers or birds. The ground is barren and rocky. Dark clouds hide the moon and lightning flashes in the distance. The Horned God stops before an old woman in tattered black robes. Icy fear fills your heart. You slide down off his back and walk toward Her. As you take Her hand, you suddenly recognize her and say, "I know you. You are the Goddess and I am not afraid." She replies, "Yes, you are my son. Only those who do not know me, fear me." As the Horned God and the Goddess embrace you, you feel the world spin around you. You take a quick breath and open your eyes. You are sitting before your campfire once again. Life and death are only passages, only changes.

Now think about your parents, your grandparents, the good times you remember, the stories about them that you've heard. Quietly begin to chant:

Old Ones hear us, Old Ones rejoice.
We are the children sending our voice.
No more destruction, no more remorse.
Dancing the heartbeat back to the source.[19]

Sit quietly by your fire and picture your ancestors in your mind one at a time. Is there an ancestor that you have unfinished business with? Is there one that you would like to tell something to or ask a question of? Take a small piece of paper and your pencil and write your message on it. Hold it tightly in your hands and visualize the ancestor it's intended for. When the energy peaks, drop it on the coals. As the paper smokes and catches fire, imagine your message going to the otherworld. Take a few slow deep breaths and walk to your altar.

Open your pocketknife. Pick up the pomegranate with your left hand saying, "This is the fruit of life which contains the seeds of death, the seeds which kept Persephone in the land of the dead." Cut the pomegranate open and let the blood-red juice run over your hand. Eat a few of the seeds. "They are bitter." Put the pomegranate down and pick up the apple saying, "This is the fruit of death which contains the seeds of life that grew in the land of Avalon." Cut the apple in half around the equator. Take a bite of one of the pieces. "It is sweet." Look at the other half of the apple saying, "This is the star of hope." Put the apple pieces down. What can be learned from these fruits? Everything that lives dies, yet from death comes new life. Life is sweet though it is brief. Death is bitter but it is not evil. Without death there can be no life. Hidden here is the great mystery, in both life and death there is hope.

Take the chalice and raise it in salute saying, "I am not the first nor will I be the last. Tonight I remember you. You are gone but never forgotten. You are ever near to my heart. I, son of _____, son of _____, son of fathers unknown salute you." Take a sip of the juice. Quietly tell one of your stories to your ancestors. Again raise the chalice in salute and take a sip. Think back over the past year, back to last October. What things have you accomplished? How have you grown up since then? What good times have you had? Raise the chalice and toast your own accomplishments. Stand and pour the rest out on the ground as a libation offering saying, "All things come from the Goddess and the Horned God and to Them they shall return." If you are indoors set the chalice back on the altar and pour it out later outside.

111

Return to your fire and sit a few moments in silence. Stand and walk to your altar. Extinguish the white candle saying, "Spirits and memories of my ancestors, I say goodbye to you for now as you go your way and I go mine." Extinguish the orange candle saying. "Lord of darkness. Lord of light. I say goodbye to you for now as you go your way and I go mine." Extinguish the black candle saying, "Lady of darkness. Lady of light. I say goodbye to you for now as you go your way and I go mine." Return to the center and face north and say, "Sustaining earth, I say goodbye to you for now as you go your way and I go mine." Turn to the west and say, "Quenching water, I say goodbye to you for now as you go your way and I go mine." Turn to the south and say, "Glowing embers, I say goodbye to you for now as you go your way and I go mine." Turn to the east and say, "Whispering breezes, I say goodbye to you for now as you go your way and I go mine."

Walk to the east side of your circle and touch the ground with your left hand. Imagine that you are taking up your circle like you would pick up a rope. Walk widdershins around your circle and imagine the glowing circle retracting into your extended left hand. Return to the center and say, "The circle is open yet unbroken. Merry did we meet and merry did we part and merry shall we meet again. Blessed be." Kneel before your fire placing the palms of your hands on the earth and ground the energy you have absorbed. Extinguish your fire, pack up your things leaving the fruit for the creatures of the woods and return home.

Unpacking the Ritual

Looking back at the ritual, the first thing I notice is that it is long. Well, any of the eight solar rituals would be longer than, say, a sitting in the woods ritual and Samhain is the most important of the eight festivals. Do your solar rituals have to be this long? By now you should know the answer to that question. Of course not. Now let's look at the details of the ritual.

I had you begin by centering and grounding. In my opinion, this is a must with any ritual, though there is more than one way to do it. Next you purified yourself by smudging with sage. You could have used a ritual bath or washed your hands and face or sprinkled yourself with salted water. There have been some rituals in which I also anointed myself on the forehead with scented oil or drew a magickal symbol on my forehead with an eyeliner pencil. It is certainly not necessary for you to do all of these things at the beginning of a ritual but you should definitely do something to ritually cleanse yourself.

Next, you cast a circle around the space where you would conduct the ritual. This time you did that by circumambulation, walking around. You could have also used your athame, wand, or staff to help you. Sometimes I walk the first time with my ritual tool casting the circle, a second time with salted water to purify the circle, and a third time with incense to charge the circle. Since it was outdoors, I assumed that the area was already clean and that sprinkling salt water wouldn't help the plants any. On the other hand, you could have just stood in the center of your circle and visualized the circle forming around you. The method you choose might depend on the festival you are celebrating, the place you use and your personal feelings.

When I invoke the Elements or Call the Quarters, I am attuning my intellect, will, emotions and senses to similar aspects of nature. In this ritual I invoked the four Elements: air, fire, water and earth. Sometimes I invoke my power animals, the elemental rulers or just the directions themselves. You can also envision yourself calling Elemental beings or guardian spirits of the directions into your circle. Whatever you choose, I find setting the call up in rhymed couplets with a few descriptive words is more effective than lengthy prose. What am I doing while I invoke the Elements? Sometimes I stand near the appropriate side of the circle looking outwards and extend my arms outwards as I call. Sometimes I also light a torch at the edge of my circle as a beacon for elemental forces. Other times I'm standing at the altar lighting a colored candle or raising a token of that element. I have also stood with the lighted candle in my left hand and my wand or athame in my right. There are many good ways to do this. Try a few of them and choose what feels right.

Like the elemental invocations, I usually write my deity invocations in rhymed couplets. You may choose to use the name of a particular deity or as I have done in this ritual simply describe the deities you are invoking. While you should not recite a long speech as an invocation, I believe it does need to be specific enough that you can visualize the form of the Goddess and God you are calling to. As with the Moon Rituals, be sure you are invoking the deity appropriate to the ritual. Since this is a Samhain ritual, I also included an invocation to the ancestors.

The second act should be the heart of your ritual. I've participated in a few rituals where the casting of the circle took longer than what we did in the circle once it was cast. Seems to me that if you go to the trouble of casting a circle and inviting the Goddess and the God to be present that you should spend some time with Them. I began with a guided meditation. You could either record it and listen to it during your ritual or read over it a few times beforehand and then just play it back in your mind. The mediation connects you with the mythology of our religion and allows you to gently ease into the work that you will do with your ancestors and yourself.

The connection to your ancestors that is especially important at Samhain is framed by a chant and the toasting. The chant further shifts your consciousness and brings the myth to a more personal level. Between them is an act of magick in which you send a message to your ancestors and a ritual that recalls Persephone's journey into the underworld. In the toasts, you are honoring your ancestors and bragging to them of your accomplishments. Drinking the juice is also a grounding technique that brings you back to the present reality.

The third act is short. The farewells are shorter than the invocations. I call them farewells because it seems presumptuous and rude to assume that I can "dismiss" the Elements and the deities as if they were my personal servants. I have chosen to do everything in the reverse of the order I did it at the beginning, undoing what I did. You can do the farewells in the same order as the invocations if you feel that widdershins movements are negative.

Having looked at a sample ritual and unpacked the parts of it, let's consider how you will write your own rituals for the other seven festivals.

Writing your own rituals

Sabbat	Theme	Colors	Activity
Yule	Birth of the God	red & green	giving gifts
Imbolc	Purification	white	healing, poetry, cleansing
Ostara	Planting	green & pink	coloring eggs, planting seeds
Beltane	Fertility	rainbow	maypole, balefire, may baskets
Litha	Greenwood Lord	green & gold	fireworks, summer picnics
Lughnasad	Harvest	gold	corn dollies, baking bread
Mabon	Balance	brown & red	thanksgiving, balance
Samhain	Death/Ending	black & gold	honoring ancestors

Which festival comes up next on your calendar? Using what you know about the purpose of the festival, the myth of the Wheel of the Year and some of the suggestions given above, begin writing your ritual. Use the Samhain ritual as a rough guide but be creative. A ritual you create yourself will be more meaningful than one from a book or website because you created it. You may choose to write one as elaborate as the Samhain Ritual or you may choose to make it much simpler.

Since the most of the Pagan festivals are celebrated under Christian guise in our culture, you can celebrate the festivals out of circle with your non-Pagan family and friends. Samhain, Yule, and Ostara are easy. Most of the Christian and secular customs of Halloween, Christmas, and Easter are of Pagan origin. So carve pumpkins, decorate the tree and color eggs. Celebrate the Wheel of the Year and have fun. Even if you have to go to church, you can remember the birth day of the Sun God and the resurrection of the plants in spring.

Imbolc is also Groundhog Day in the United States. While there isn't a big celebration over this one your mom isn't going to be mad if you clean your room and give her a pot of early blooming crocus, hyacinths or daffodils. Mayday isn't that big nowadays, either. Few towns have Maypole dances anymore but you can observe it again with flowers. A May Basket is a small basket of fresh-picked wildflowers. Can you think of anyone who needs their day brightened by an anonymous basket of flowers? Summer Solstice is close enough to the American Independence Day that fireworks (if they are legal where you live) should be available. A picnic or day at the beach followed by roman candles and Catherine wheels is an appropriate way to celebrate the peak of the Sun's power. For Lammas I always bake some "from scratch" cornbread using my mother's secret recipe. It's really not hard. If you aren't confident that you can bake bread, you could plan a picnic with roast corn and watermelon for your family or group of friends. By Fall Equinox it's football season (in the U.S. anyway) and in some places county fairs are held as the weather gets cooler. Both of these are ways you can celebrate the harvest and the time of balance. Whether your sabbat ritual is done within a cast circle or not, your celebration can be a celebration nevertheless.

The Great Rite

Before I leave off writing about the myth and ritual of the Wheel of the Year I would be remiss if I did not mention the Great Rite. In the physical world, most life comes from the sexual union of male and female. In the myth, life comes from the union of the Goddess and the Horned God. This was enacted in ritual in ancient times by the sexual union of the priestess and the priest who represented the Goddess and the Horned God. In modern Paganism this is usually enacted symbolically with ritual tools.

The Great Rite is done toward the end of the second act of a ritual and is often linked with what is called Cakes and Ale or The Simple Feast. The purpose of the Great Rite is to re-enact the union of the Goddess and the Horned God. The purpose of Cakes and Ale is to give thanks for the gifts that result from that union and to ground some of the energy raised during the ritual.

You will need your athame, your chalice, a small bottle of juice, your pentacle and a piece of bread. Pour the juice into the chalice, put the bread on the pentacle, and put both on your altar. Take the chalice in your left hand and the athame in your right. Lower the athame into a chalice saying, "As the blade is to the male, so the cup is to the female; and when joined, they become one and are a great blessing." Put the chalice down and pick up the pentacle. Trace a pentagram in the air over the bread with your athame and say these words, "Blessed be this bread, gift of Earth and the Sun." Put the athame down and say, "May you never hunger." Break the bread into pieces and eat some. Put the pentacle down and pick up the chalice saying, "May you never thirst." Drink some of the juice. Pick up the pentacle and the chalice. Raise them high saying, "As all things come from the Goddess and the Horned God so to them they must return." Pour the juice onto the ground and sprinkle the bread as an offering.

God of the Harvest

The Wheel of the Year isn't just something you do inside a magick circle. Keeping a small garden is one way you can experience the Wheel as your ancestors did.

I'm going to describe a possible garden plan. Your actual garden plan will depend on the space you have available. The sorts of plants you can cultivate will depend on the climate where you live. I can not possibly include all the specific answers so you should go to the library and read the books that are available and specific to your area. You should talk to other gardeners in your area to find out what they plant and how they grow it successfully. One excellent inexpensive resource is *The Old Farmer's Almanac*. You can find it in most bookstores and online.

The time to begin preparing your garden is autumn about the time leaves begin to fall. I prefer to plant a garden in beds rather than rows because the growing plants shade the soil, cutting down on weeding. I also mulch heavily for the same reason and mulching also helps the soil retain moisture so I don't have to water as much. Most vegetables require at least six hours of sunlight so look for the sunniest part of your yard. While your garden will need water it also doesn't need to become a bog every time it rains. Look for a well-drained spot that doesn't have standing water a day after a rain. Mark off a rectangle with stakes and string three feet wide and as long as you intend to make your garden. Nine feet is plenty long enough to begin with.

Cover the grass with a layer of newspaper four or five sheets thick. Water it and cover with compost. As leaves fall, rake them and pile them on top. I've made it a habit to "harvest" the leaves that my neighbors so thoughtfully bag and place on the curb with their trash. Water the leaves occasionally to keep them damp but not soggy. Let your garden rest through the winter, checking it occasionally to see if it needs more water. By spring, the leaves should have composted somewhat and your garden will be ready to plant.

Spend the winter choosing what you will plant and where you will plant when spring comes. Choose a mix of vegetables, herbs, flowers and greenery. Depending on your local climate, work your planting into one of the three planting festivals.

After all danger of frost has passed and the soil has warmed sufficiently, plant your seeds during the two weeks of the waxing moon. I use my wand both to measure how far apart to plant the seeds and to make the holes in the earth to plant them. Kneel at the edge of your garden. Center and ground. Hold your wand in your right hand so you can use it to measure the depth of planting and the distance between plantings. Hold the seeds in your left hand. Touch the seeds with your wand. Visualize the power and energy of the Horned God flowing down your arms through your wand into the seeds. Rake the mulch aside and make a hole in the earth with your wand. Quickly drop a seed in saying, "As the wand is to man so the furrow is to woman. With the power of Horned God, I plant these seeds into Mother Earth." Turn your wand to measure the distance to the next hole and continue planting. When you finish planting one row or one type of seeds, use your wand to brush the soil filling in the seed holes. If you are transplanting plants rather than planting seeds, use the same ritual process. Use a small trowel to make the hole and lightly touch the plant with your wand after it is in the ground saying, "Little plant, green and strong. Grow in Mother Earth where you belong." After you have finished planting, give the seeds or young plants a drink of water, clean your tools and put them away. Record your progress in your Book of Shadows.

Having planted your garden, the work is not over. In coming weeks and months you will need to weed and water your garden. Water your garden in the evening before sunset. Do your weeding during the waning moon. Add more mulch and you won't need to weed and water as often. Harvest your garden as plants ripen and as you do give thanks to the Horned God and the Goddess for their gifts. Depending on your location, you may do a second planting in the late summer or early fall. Use the fruits of your garden in your celebrations of the three harvest festivals.

In this and the previous chapters you have learned how to enact the mythology of our religion through ritual and through practical actions. The next chapter focuses on your transformation from a boy into a man.

Chapter 6

Your Passage into Manhood

If you can keep your head when all about you
Are losing theirs and blaming it on you;
If you can trust yourself when all men doubt you,
But make allowance for their doubting too;
If you can wait and not be tired by waiting,
Or, being lied about, don't deal in lies,
Or, being hated, don't give way to hating,
And yet don't look too good, nor talk too wise; ...
If you can talk with crowds and keep your virtue,
Or walk with kings - nor lose the common touch;
If neither foes nor loving friends can hurt you;
If all men count with you, but none too much;
If you can fill the unforgiving minute
With sixty seconds' worth of distance run -
Yours is the Earth and everything that's in it,
And - which is more - you'll be a Man my son![20]
Rudyard Kipling

Stumbling into manhood

One of the things I remember my father saying to me when I was
a young boy was, "One day you are going to wake up and you're
going to be grown". While I knew he didn't mean it literally, I
remember waking up a lot of mornings with those words
running through my mind. It wasn't like I really expected it to be
that sudden but I kept wondering when that magick of "being
grown" was going to happen to me. Like many men, I stumbled
my way into manhood, not ever feeling that I was there yet.

In ancient times, boys learned to hunt with their fathers and the other men. Puberty came a few years later than it does today, and shortly afterwards a boy went through his rite of passage into manhood. The rite involved a separation from his mother, an in-between time of testing alone and a reincorporation back into the tribe as a man. It was more than just a candlelight ritual with speeches. A real transformation had occurred.

I remember going to Methodist confirmation class for a week and learning all about the church and my responsibilities to it. I was proud to stand before the congregation on Confirmation Sunday and promise to support the church with my prayers, presence, gifts and service, but when the ceremony was over I was still as much a boy as before. I can say the same for getting my driver's license, graduating from high school, registering to vote and registering for the draft. Even when I graduated from college and got a full-time job, I didn't feel grown. There was never any point where I definitely knew, now I am a man.

I believe that a rite of passage initiating a boy into manhood is something critical that's missing from modern society. Why do so many teenage guys do obviously risky things like drinking until they pass out, experimenting with street drugs, dangerous driving, joining gangs and extreme sports. I believe these are mainly attempts to make a break with childhood and parents, prove themselves and initiate themselves into manhood. Even harmless things like hair styles, clothing and music can be used as ways to separate yourself from your parents and declare your independence. The problem with this is that some of these things are dangerous and none of them, even the harmless ones, work to transform you into a man.

When I was writing this book I had conversations with several men about rites of passage into manhood, what a 21st century rite might be like, and whether a boy could successfully self-initiate. The most helpful were an Australian man called Wyrmwood and my minister, Rev. Jose Ballester. These are some of the things we agreed were important. A successful rite of passage is critical.

Without one a boy will either try to self-initiate with disastrous results or will enter adulthood without a clear sense of what being a man is supposed to be about and without a clear sense of having become a man. The rite needs to be more than just a ceremony. It needs to be something that makes a real change in the boy's life. A period of learning is something that was a part of earlier rites of passage and it's even more important today. Since puberty and full adult independence are now separated by some eight to ten years, a single rite of passage like in ancient times is not enough. Two rites, one at the beginning of adolescence that deals with puberty, and one at the end of adolescence to finalize the passage into full adult manhood are necessary. If you are fortunate enough to have a Pagan father, talk to him now about arranging your Rites of Passage into Manhood. While your father or your adult male mentor is the ideal person to supervise the Rites of Passage, in the absence of adult male initiators I believe self-initiation is possible.

Separation from Childhood

Your first Rite of Passage deals with the physical beginning of manhood at puberty. Even if you went through puberty a few years ago it is important that you both celebrate and take responsibility for the changes that have occurred. During the separation phase you will be separating yourself from habits and behaviors of childhood.

In some hunter-gatherer societies boys were ritually kidnapped from their mothers and carried away by the men for their rite of passage. In modern society, this is not possible. Even if there were a committee of men to do the kidnapping, it's not possible to learn everything you need to know in one period of seclusion. In addition to this, in modern society the gender roles are not as sharply defined as in ancient times. In many families both parents share what were traditionally tasks done by the mother. Rather than being a physical one-time event, part of the modern separation is a process of becoming less dependent on your parents. This doesn't mean you don't love your parents or care about them. It just means that you aren't a little boy anymore.

You can not accomplish this all at once but you can begin. At dark moon use a fire scrying ritual to decide which things you will focus on. Your goal is to make a short list of three or fewer things which you depend on your parents to do for you that you can begin to do for yourself. Do you get yourself up in the morning or does one of your parents wake you up like you are still a little kid? Do you make and change your own bed or does your they do it? Do you clean your room and keep it reasonably clean or do you expect them to do it and complain when they finally do? Do you do your own laundry or do you expect your parents to not only pick up your dirty clothes, but wash and dry them, fold them and put them away for you? Are there other things around the house that your parents do for you that you could do? OK, so your family has a maid who does all this. Does that keep you from doing it? After you have your short list, write your plans for the month in your Book of Shadows. How will you accomplish these things? When the Sun rises on your next day accept the responsibilities you have chosen and take another step toward manhood. Don't look at these as chores but as part of your rite of passage.

By the time of the next waning moon you will have been shouldering these new responsibilities for three weeks. Now it is time for the Cutting the Cords Ritual. You will need a green cord or ribbon long enough to tie around your waist like a belt, and a red cord or ribbon about three feet long for each of the things that you have taken responsibility for this month. You will also need your cauldron and pocketknife. Center yourself and create sacred space invoking the Elements. Kneel before your cauldron and invoke the goddess Cerridwen. As you tie the green cord around your waist, invoke the Horned God. Take one of the red cords and hold it tightly in your right hand. Visualize the dependency on your parents that you have severed this month. Speak its name aloud. Tie the cord to the cauldron and to the green cord that is around your waist. Do the same for the other red cords. When all the cords are tied say, "This is what was. I was a boy." Open your knife and gripping it tightly in your right hand cut the red cords saying, "This is what is now. I am becoming a man." When all the cords are cut, burn the ones attached to the cauldron and keep the ones still attached to the green cord as a reminder of who you are becoming. Wait until the next dark moon to choose new responsibilities to take on. If you slip backwards toward dependency on your parents add those to the list of possible things to take on during the next moon cycle.

In ancient times boys were taught how to be men by their fathers and the other adult males of the tribe. One of the reasons for the rocky passage into manhood many boys experience is that this bonding/mentoring does not happen. The year I taught at the alternative high school, I listened while my students talked about their fathers. One of them expressed his rage at his father who had deserted him and didn't even visit or send presents on holidays. The others agreed and told similar stories of how their fathers had not only never been there for them but had never been there at all. Maybe there were good reasons why they had failed their sons but regardless of their reasons, their sons were hurt and angry. It is a small wonder that in their anger they had done things that had caused them to be expelled from regular school. No one should go through life with this kind of anger bottled up inside them.

My own father went to work every day and was home every night and every weekend. I have a lot of good memories of him and still use many of the things he taught me, but there was always a barrier between us. It wasn't until after I was in college and he got me a summer job at the plant that I really understood what he actually did all day at work. It was years later before we had much fun together. He was often harsh, belittling me and the things I was interested in. I think he was disappointed that I wasn't interested in or good at sports like he had been. Maybe he thought that he was helping to make me tough. Maybe he was. I'm glad that I had the chance to reconcile with him before he died. I hope that whatever your father is like and what your relationship with him is like that you will find the way to reconcile yourself to him and him to you.

I believe that it is vitally important for you as a young man to have a father or father figure, an adult male mentor, whom you can confide in and learn from. If your father has failed you in major ways then you must find ways not to carry anger toward him around with you all the time. You do not need to forgive and forget but you do need acknowledge your anger and deal with it. Recognize the feelings you have for what they are: your real and honest feelings. A waning moon ritual is useful in turning loose of them, as is a ritual bath.

Your next task is to spend some time thinking and writing what you know about your father. What is your father like? How would you describe him? What do you admire about him? What things about him do you not admire? What do you know of his personal history? What does he enjoy doing? Add this to your Book of Shadows.

Then begin to talk with him, assuming that he is around to talk to. If your biological father is not available, go to the man who has been a father to you. If you can't think of anyone, use the fire scrying ritual to discover three men whom you could go to as if they were your father, perhaps a stepfather, grandfather, uncle, teacher or coach. Why three? Three is a good number because chances are that one or more of these men won't be the one who will stand in for your biological father.

Pick a time when you think he will be able to give you his undivided attention. Perhaps you could even make a sort of appointment to talk to him. Ask him like a man, directly.

Something like, "Dad, do you have some time? I have something I want to ask you." He will be surprised and a little flattered that you want to ask him something, and more than a little curious about what it might be. What things do you want to know from him? You need to make a short list. They might be things like: Who were his father and his grandfather? What were they like? When he was a boy, what did he want to be when he grew up? What were his dreams? How did he meet your mother? How did he feel about becoming a father? How did he learn about sex? Was he embarrassed the first time he bought a condom? What does he think being a man is all about? Obviously you can't ask all these questions at once. Pick a few and realize that these questions will lead to other questions. If he asks you similar questions, answer honestly. Listen carefully and later record his thoughts in your Book of Shadows. As with taking responsibility for yourself, bonding with your father is not a one-time thing. Hopefully the first chat will lead to other chats and real bonding.

It may be that your father or mentor has given you or will give you a special token from his life. I have a couple of my dad's rings, his knife, his tools and a buckeye seed that his grandfather gave him. You may choose to wear, carry, or display your tokens in a special place or put them away somewhere safe. Use them to remind yourself of your father and your bonds to him.

One of the other things you should begin doing in your Book of Shadows is building your family tree. To connect with your ancestors, you have to know who they were and something about their lives. Start with yourself, your birth date and place. Next, in pyramid fashion below, write your mother's and father's names, their dates and places of birth and their marriage date and place. Below them, put your grandparents and information about them. By talking with older members of your family, you should be able to go back as far as your great grandparents or maybe a generation further back. Visit your local public library and ask about the genealogy section. They will have resources to help you dig deeper and organize the information that you find. You are looking for more than just names and dates. You are looking for personal histories. If you are being raised by someone other than your biological parents, you may choose to list them and their ancestors as your own rather than your biological parents. At some point you will be unable go back further. The rest of your lineage is a mystery. These are your fathers and mothers unknown.

As a young Pagan you can call on your ancestors for guidance and support. For this ancestor ritual you will need a black altar cloth, a quartz crystal, copal or frankincense incense, a small bowl, a bottle of water and a small white candle. This kind of ritual is usually done at Samhain but if you need to connect with your ancestors at some other time then your need outweighs the traditional timing.

Make a list of your ancestors, living and dead, as far back as you can. Go to your sacred place and set up your altar with the crystal in the center of your altar, point up, and the bowl of water between you and the crystal. Light a white candle and place it on the north side of the altar. Create sacred space. Invoke Cerridwen and the Horned God. Sit on the south side of your altar and gaze into the crystal. Call upon your ancestors with these or similar words, "Fathers of my father and mothers of my mother. My beloved ancestors stand before me now and share your wisdom. I am your son, _____. I am the son of (your father's name), the son of (your grandfather's name), the son of (your great grandfather's name), the son of fathers unknown… Come to me now." Continue to repeat these words while staring into the crystal until your consciousness shifts and your vision blurs. Gently close your eyes or if you are good at scrying, leave them open.

Visualize your departed ancestors standing in a line that recedes into the distance. One by one they walk toward you. Do you recognize anyone? If you do, greet them by name. Do they have any wisdom for you at this time? Ask them any questions you wish. Sometimes you will receive an answer right away. Maybe your answer will come later.

When you have finished the time with your ancestors, pick up the bowl of water and lifting it upwards in salute say, "My beloved ancestors, thank you for your continued presence with me. I drink in your wisdom." Lower the bowl to your lips and drink some of the water. Raise the bowl again and say, "My beloved ancestors, may there ever be peace between us." Tip the bowl and pour out the rest of the water as an offering to your ancestors. Now, say farewell to Cerridwen and the Horned God. Return to ordinary space and ground any excess energy. Whether you must pack up your things and go home or whether you spend the night outside, before you go to sleep, record your impressions in your Book of Shadows.

Welcoming Changes

Puberty is a time of major changes in your body. It is a time when you should begin paying more attention to your body, listening to it and taking care of it. Remember, your body is sacred. As your hormones kick in your scent changes and becomes that of an adult male. This sometimes happens almost overnight. Bathe or shower daily and after exercise even if you don't think you need to. If you don't already, start using deodorant. You may have to try several brands until you find the one that works best for you. The high level of testosterone during puberty makes your face oily and leads to acne if you don't pay more attention to your skin than you did as a boy. Make it a habit to wash your face twice a day with a good facial cleanser and apply one of the many over-the-counter acne products to problem areas.

Exercise is important at any age but especially now. When you get up in the morning spend just a few minutes doing stretches. This will help lengthen your muscles which can get tight because your bones are growing so fast. It will also get your blood flowing and reduce the chance of injury. Plan some time every day for aerobic exercise that gets your heart and lungs going. Running, jogging, speed walking, bicycling, swimming, or calisthenics are examples of this kind of exercise. The third type of exercise you should be doing is resistance exercise, either lifting weights or doing exercise in which you are using your muscles to lift your body's own weight, things like push-ups, sit-ups, and knee bends. Pick a time. Make it a habit or ritual. Keep a record of the exercises you do each day, your progress, and make regular measurements of your physical growth. With all the testosterone coursing through your blood, you should be able to build muscles with only a little regular work, but don't get impatient if your muscles don't get huge over night. It's not that you are trying to be a bodybuilder. You are getting your body in shape and becoming more and more a true son of the Horned God. As you exercise, remember the words of the Horned God, "I am He who is the taste of salt upon your tongue."[21]

They say, "You are what you eat." I think you are more than just what you eat but there is some truth to the saying. Without becoming a fanatic about it, pay attention to what you eat, how much you eat and when you eat it. Most guys get that bottomless pit appetite just before or during the early months of puberty. It's normal. Your body is growing fast and needs more food. Be sure you are getting lots of protein, vitamins and minerals, and not just a lot of sugar, starch, salt and fats. Learn how to prepare yourself nutritious snacks for after-school and late-night munchies. If you find that you can grab a handful of flab at your middle, drinking water with a little lemon added instead sodas may be all you need to get rid of it. You'll look better and feel better if you keep your weight within the normal ranges for your height. Silently thank the Horned God as you eat and remember that it is, "He whose bones grace your every meal."[22]

Menarche, the beginning of menstruation, marks the beginning of a girl's puberty. Often boys reach puberty less prepared for all the physical and emotional changes than girls do. For boys the beginning of puberty is less definite. First semen, whether it happens during masturbation or as a result of a wet dream, is much more private, even secretive. I began puberty shortly after I turned thirteen and it was months before anyone but me realized that anything had taken place. I wasn't sure myself what it was supposed to mean. Times have changed and I'm sure you are more informed that I was. Just be sure that you do have accurate and correct information about your growing sexuality. Don't forget about your father or mentor as a source for this information.

Ours is a fertility religion. In nature there is a continuing creation of life through the sexual union of male and female. Plants pollinate. Animals and humans have sex. That is how "higher" organisms on Earth reproduce. The Wheel of the Year tells the story of the very sexual relationship between the Goddess and the Horned God. Pagan attitudes toward sex and sexuality are quite different from the dominant religions of the west. They view sex as sinful at worst and a necessary evil at best. As Pagans we know that sex is neither sinful nor shameful. It is a sacred force and a sacred act, the gift of the Goddess and the embodiment of the Horned God. It is a powerful creative force and a source of great joy and pleasure.

Does all this mean that since you are a Pagan it's OK to have sex with your girlfriend or boyfriend or whoever is available at the moment? The answer is found in the words of the Rede, "An' it harm none, do as you will." Getting a sexually transmitted disease, especially one that is incurably fatal, is definitely harming someone, you. Creating a new life that you are not ready to be responsible for definitely harms others, your partner, the child that you are not ready to be a father to and yourself. Unless you are mature enough to buy and properly use a condom every time, you can not have sex with another person without causing harm.

Beyond just the physical aspects of sex, I have said that Pagans view sex as sacred. Not sinful but truly, deeply sacred. What does this mean? The best explanation I've heard was one told to me by a fourteen-year-old Pagan called Ravenlore: "First let it be noted that Pagans are supposed to have self-control. Before any spell is cast, before any ritual, self-control should be taught. Now, I have had the urge for sex more times than I can count. Yeah, I'm bad, I know, but I have yet to actually have sex. The craving for the flesh is one of the most tempting encounters anyone will ever have. Now, I believe that sex is sacred and also very powerful. It is a blessing to be able to perform and should be treated with much respect. With that said, sex should be performed only in the presence of an immense, almost overwhelming feeling of love. All other instances, I believe, are not suitable for sex. There is no age limit on love but there is a certain maturity that must be reached before someone can even realize what love is, and when sex is appropriate."[23] I would add that there also must be a commitment to one another and the maturity to be able to live up to that commitment.

So what about masturbation? Well, does it harm anyone else? No. Does it harm you? No. Does it help relieve the overpowering build-up of sexual pressure? Yes. Does it feel really good? Are you kidding? Yes! Then there is nothing wrong with masturbating for the sheer pleasure of it or to release the almost unbearable urge for sex that most teenage males feel. It is not only a totally normal thing to do but is a sacred gift.

Now about sexual orientation, unlike some other religions, it's really not an issue with Pagans. Regardless of whether you are straight, gay, bisexual, transgendered, or aren't sure, you are a son of the Goddess and the Horned God. One of the goals of Paganism is to become more fully who you are. This includes who you are as far as your sexual orientation. This is quite different from the religions that insist that you need to change and become something else since what you are is not acceptable.

Most guys start off by assuming they are heterosexual. About ninety percent of us are. Some of the gay men I've talked to have told me that they knew they were gay at a very early age or said that they always knew. Others weren't sure until much later. There is no rush to figure it out and declare your sexual orientation. There is also no need for you to grapple with your sexual orientation or when and how to come out alone. Consider contacting one of these groups: PFLAG, GLBST Club, Metropolitan Community Church or Unitarian Universalist Church. The thing is, be who you are and love who you love and know that it is more than just OK. It is sacred.

Your Puberty Ritual

For this ritual marking your passage from childhood to adolescence to be effective, you should have already begun doing the work of cutting the cords of childhood with your parents, seeking the wisdom of your father (or adult male mentor) and your ancestors and accepting responsibility for your budding sexuality. If your father or adult male mentor is Pagan, he should work with you to write and carry out your Puberty Ritual. If you are working alone, here is an example of a ritual you might use.

You will need a green altar cloth, chalice, pentacle, salt, water, incense, a red votive candle, a token from your childhood, a token of your father, some acorns, a small box to put your childhood token in and a small pouch to put the tokens of your father in. This ritual should ideally be part of an overnight outdoors vigil but if this is impossible it could be adapted to fit your circumstances. Spend time reading the words of this ritual so that you can almost say them from memory. Feel free as always to change or adapt them.

Set up your campsite and altar. Put about a teaspoon full of salt on the pentacle on the north side, the incense on the east side, the candle on the south side and the chalice of water on the west side. Breathe deeply, center, and ground yourself. Spend some time in quiet thought and meditation, think about your life, your childhood, the changes that are upon you and your path as a man. When you are ready, light the incense and candle. If you are doing this outdoors, your vigil fire would be behind you.

When you are ready, walk to the east side of your area and begin to walk deosil around your altar saying, "Here I cast a circle of light. Nothing enter but love. Nothing emerge but love." Imagine a glowing path of light where your feet have walked.

When you have circled the altar three times, stop at the eastern side of your circle and say, "Guardians of the East, I call on you as my mind enters the time of great change. Come and teach me the ancient knowledge as I become a man". Walk to the south side of your circle and say, "Guardians of the South, I call on you as my path enters the time of great change. Come and show me the way as I become a man." Walk to the west side of your circle and say, "Guardians of the West, I call on you as my emotions enter the time of great change. Come and calm my feelings as I become a man." Walk to the north side of your circle and say, "Guardians of the North, I call on you as my body enters the time of great change. Come and let me be comfortable with my changing body as I become a man."

Return to the center and stand before your altar with your arms crossed over your chest, your hands in the Horned God position and say, "Come to me, Horned One, as I become man, and I shall always keep my purpose clear remembering that Yours is a path of the heart. I shall not forget Mother Earth, how She supports me and gives me life. I will work to heal Her and to learn Her wisdom. Horned One, thank you that I am becoming a man."

Pick up the token of your childhood. Hold it tightly in your right hand and say, "This is a token of my childhood. Though I put it away as I enter manhood, its memory is every with me." Put the token in the box or bag and seal it shut. You will put it away somewhere safe when you return home. Pick up the severed ribbons from your Cutting the Cords Ritual, hold them tightly and say, "These are a token of how I am no longer dependent on my parents as I was as a little boy." Place the cords on the altar next to your childhood token. Put them in a safe place when you return home so you can be reminded of the new role you have assumed. Pick up the token from your father and your ancestors and place them in the pouch. Hold it tightly in your right hand and say, "These are tokens of my father and his fathers, as I wear them about my neck may I ever be reminded of the wisdom I receive from them." Hang the cord of the pouch around your neck. Whether you choose to wear the pouch all the time or only on special occasions is your choice. Pick up a handful of acorns, hold them tightly and say, "These seeds are the token of my manhood. I accept responsibility for planting and tending these seeds as I accept the responsibilities of manhood." Place the seeds on your altar. When you return home carefully plant and tend them as detailed in the previous chapter.

Remove your clothes, fold them and place them near your feet. Touch the water with your right index finger saying, "Element of Water, be clean for this rite." Touch the salt with your right index finger saying, "Element of Earth, be charged for this rite." Pick up your pentacle with your right hand and pour the salt into the water. Put the pentacle down and pick up the chalice with your left hand. Dip the fingers of your right hand into the water and as you place your hand on the top of your head say, "Bless me, Father, for I am Your child." Dip your fingers into the water again as you touch each part of your body in turn saying, "Bless my eyes for they are Your eyes, and I will clearly see my path. Bless my nose for it is Your nose, and I will smell the essence of the wild. Bless my lips for they are Your lips, and I will speak the truth with kindness. Bless my mine heart for it is Your heart and I will be true to my own self. Bless my penis for it is Your life-giving organ and I will bring forth both life and pleasure. Bless my knees for they are Your knees and I will stand proud and unshaken. Bless my feet for they are Your feet and I will walk on my chosen path. Bless me, Father, for I am Your child, now and always."

Put the chalice down and stand for a moment and look at your body. How has it changed since you began puberty? What changes are yet to occur? You are becoming a man. Not fully a man yet but becoming. You are a son of the Horned God. Pick up your clothes and put them back on.

Kneel before your altar and say, "I do not say farewell to you, Guardians of the Elements, for you are always with me. I do not say farewell to you, Horned God, for You are always with me. My circle is now open yet ever unbroken. Blessed be." Place your hands on the ground palm down and ground the excess energy.

As you sit beside your vigil fire, spend some time writing letters to your mother and father or your adult mentors. Mention something you have learned from them, thank them for something specific that they have done for you and tell the story of about one of the good times you had together. Thank them for being your parents or mentor. When you get sleepy, bank your fire and go to sleep. In the morning, break camp and return home, not a child any more.

If you have a supportive Pagan family they will welcome you back from your ritual and work to reincorporate you into the family in your new role. The absence of such support is without a doubt the weakest part of a modern Rite of Passage. You can not change your family but you can change yourself. In the coming days pay attention to how your relationship to the members of your family has changed. Do you still quarrel with your brother or sister, or do you find ways to work out your disagreements? Do you still depend on your parents for things you could do for yourself? Are there ways you can further build your relationship with your father or mentor? Are there more things you can learn from him? How are you taking further responsibility for your actions and taking your place in the world as a man?

Milestones and Tasks

Between puberty and manhood there are a number of milestones to reach, tasks to accomplish and the great decision as to what comes beyond. Among these milestone are falling in love for the first time and breaking up, finding and keeping a part-time job, getting a driver's license, registering to vote and graduating from high school. In addition to the milestones of growing up, I challenge you to take up a series of tasks.

While you are in school your main job is your school work. I challenge you to go beyond what you are required to do and become a scholar. Pick a topic of interest to you. Learn all you can about it. Keep a record of the sources with the goal of writing an essay or term paper based on your research and experiences. This is not something you are going to finish in a few days or even a few months.

The bardic arts include music, poetry and storytelling. I challenge you to learn to play a musical instrument or another one if you are already proficient with one. Study the various kinds of poetry, their rhyme and meter. Choose a few poems to memorize. Devote a section of your Book of Shadows to poetry, your own. Become familiar with the folk tales of various countries and the characteristics of oral literature. Memorize and recite a folk tale. Consider writing or adapting one of your own.

Service to the tribe and the family has always been an integral part of what was expected of a man. I believe that our mythology, ethics and understanding of ritual give us a unique responsibility to work for economic, social and environmental justice in our community and our nation. I agree with Rev. Jose Ballester that if we are content just to study our mythology and do our rituals but do not use them to enable us to speak truth to power we will choke on our mythology and our rituals.[24] Get involved with local groups who are working for racial and economic equality. Get involved with local groups that are working for women's rights. Get involved with local groups that are working for equal rights for gay, lesbian and transgender persons. Get involved with local environmental and conservation groups. Sign the petitions. March in the parades. Get involved in the political process for justice and equality. When you are old enough, register and vote. The truth is that a dedicated person like you can make a difference. A fairly small number of dedicated people have always been what has brought about change.

The last, yet most important task that I challenge you to attempt is that of finding your bliss. Various authors have defined one's bliss differently but they agree that it is that thing that excites you and makes you feel like you have accomplished something. It is your life's mission. You will be working at a job of some kind forty or more hours a week for some forty-five years. Better that this be a job you find rewarding than one whose only reward is a paycheck. I challenge you to begin now looking for your bliss and as you become a man to follow it if you can.

Questing and Initiation

As I said in a previous chapter, I view initiation as something the God and the Goddess do for you when you are ready rather than a ritual that you do, like joining a fraternity or graduating from school. However, initiation is more likely to occur when you are you are seeking it and are in a state of ritual consciousness. It can happen during meditation or a walk in the woods, but it usually involves something longer and more intense.

As you practice your religion, you are going to spend quite a bit of time in the outdoors. You are going on longer and more strenuous hikes and campouts. You will become quite proficient in your outdoor skills. On some of these longer overnight treks you may decide to seek initiation by the Horned God and the Goddess. My suggestions as to how you might do this are inspired by the Native American "Crying for a Vision" or Vision Quest. What I present here is not an authentic Native American ceremony nor is it an adaptation of one. I am not authorized to do that. It is a purely Neopagan ritual that resembles the Native American ceremony only in that the seeker goes into the wilderness for a number of days to fast and pray. Both use incense and dance to achieve ritual consciousness. Both the magick circle and the medicine wheel are quartered circles. I feel these are an example of spiritual convergence rather than a matter of spiritual plagiarism.

When you choose the number of days you will go on your quest, don't say something like, "I will be gone three days." because if you can't last the whole three days you will feel like a failure. Rather say, "I will not be gone more than three days." That way your parents will know to start looking for you if you are gone longer but you won't feel like you have failed if you have to come back sooner.

Plan to travel light with only what you can carry. You will need a change of clothes in case you get wet. You will also need your sleeping bag and ground cloth, a towel and wash cloth, your poncho, fire starting kit, your compass, drinking cup and pocketknife. Bring a half gallon of drinking water for each day or a water filtration bottle if a stream is near the site. As far as ritual tools, you are traveling light. You will need sage, sweetgrass, cedar, four strips of cloth - one for each of the colors of the Elements and your Spirit Bag. You may want to bring your athame or wand and a token of the Horned God.

Pack your things the day before your departure. As you pack them smudge them with sage. On the morning of your departure, rise early, bathe, smudge yourself with sage and eat a light breakfast. Don't consume any caffeine or sugar. Say goodbye and hit the road. Assuming that you have to drive to your destination, drive in silence. If you stop along the way, speak very little. This is the separation phase of your quest.

When you arrive at the place you have chosen set up your ritual camp. Place your sleeping bag near the center of your space. Collect firewood to last the night and build a small fire lay about three feet to the east of your sleeping bag. Place the altar cloth on the ground between the fire and your sleeping bag and put your ritual supplies on it. Tie the strips of cloth to a branch or stick equal distances from altar cloth in each of the cardinal directions.

Now stand at the foot of your sleeping bag facing east. Center and ground. Light your sage smudge stick and walk a widdershins spiral outward to the perimeter of your space. Make three circuits around the perimeter and stop at the north cloth. Return to the center. Extinguish your sage. Walk a deosil spiral moving inward three times around your circle. When you reach the center turn and walk to the eastern cloth and invoke the Spirits of Air to help you in your rite. Continue to walk deosil around your circle invoking each of the Elements as you go. When you arrive back at the north, walk a deosil spiral back to the center. Light your fire sprinkling sweetgrass on it as it blazes up, and invoke the Goddess and the Horned God. This begins the liminal phase, the in-between time and the time of testing.

Sit for a while before your fire observing your surroundings. Begin your prayer rounds by sprinkling cedar on your fire. Then walk to the east and ask for clarity of mind. Walk around the circle stopping at the south and ask for strength of will, the west and ask for steady emotions and finally stop at the north and ask for sharp senses. Return to the center and ask the Goddess and the Horned God for a vision. Having finished one round of prayers, begin again by going to the east and repeating your prayer. Take your time. When you pray with your eyes open, notice the details of your surroundings in a detached way. If a bird or plant or cloud catches your attention watch it. Examine it closely with all your senses. The things of nature that you hear and see now are not just natural things but are doorways to the sacred. Be open to what they can teach you. Continue to make your rounds and keep your fire burning.

When you get tired, stop and rest sitting on your sleeping bag before your fire. When you get thirsty, stop and drink some water. It is important that you not become dehydrated. If you need to relieve yourself, walk beyond your space and take care of your needs. Occasionally you will have to stop and gather more wood. Be sure you have a good supply before dark. Do not worry about leaving your space. You have created a place to meet the sacred but have not cast a circle around it.

When night falls, continue your circuit of prayers until you become tired then sit before your fire and meditate. Whether you stay up all night to keep a vigil or sleep seeking answers in your dreams, take time to go deep within. In the morning, wash your face, drink some water, take care of your needs, gather wood, build up your fire and begin your rounds of prayer. Spend your resting time looking at the soil at your feet, the plants around you, the birds and animals that pass through your space and the clouds that drift overhead. They could be the messengers of your answers. Work collecting firewood for the night. On the last night of your quest, you will be tired, almost exhausted. Say an evening prayer to the Goddess and the Horned God and go to sleep.

On the last morning of your quest, wash your face, drink your fill of the water and take care of your needs. Return to your fire, sprinkle cedar on the coals and blow on them until the cedar smokes. Stand downwind and allow the smoke to surround your body. Allow the sweet cedar smoke to energize your tired body. Strip off your dirty clothes and wash your body in some of the water you have left. When you have put on your clean clothes, stand, center and ground, then thank the Goddess and the Horned God. Walk to the north cloth, remove it, and thank the Spirits of Earth. Walk to the west, the south, and the east stopping to remove each cloth and thank the Spirits of the Elements. Take a last long look around your space then ground.

Now, put out your fire, roll up your sleeping bag and pack up to go home. As you travel back home, think about the lessons you've learned and the answers you've received. Perhaps, you will be able to share some of them with your parents. If your quest is successful you will return a slightly different person than the one who left. The process of settling back in and finding your new place in things is the reincorporation phase of your quest.

It may require more than one quest before the Goddess and the Horned God choose to initiate you. There are also other reasons why you may decide to go on a quest. Consider the deep question of who you are. WHO are you? Who ARE you? Who are YOU? How is who you are defined? This is a worthy answer to quest for. What vision will carry you into manhood? This is another worthy question. Sometimes the point of a quest is to question your answers rather than just answer your questions. You may want to take your Book of Shadows with you on your quests or decide to leave it at home. Be sure you record your experiences in it.

Sacrifice and Offerings

Sacrifice and offerings are part of worship in most religions but do modern Pagans make sacrifice as part of their worship? Pagans at least as far back as Doreen Valiente have felt that the Goddess does not require sacrifice. However, in the Charge of the God we are called to learn the secrets of love and sacrifice. I think part of the confusion comes from the multiple meaning of the word sacrifice. One meaning of the word has to do with ritual sacrifice. This is when an animal or even human is killed in payment for a sin that the worshiper has committed. As Pagans we don't believe that our Gods are angry with us. We also believe that we must take responsibility for our actions. We can't avoid the consequences of our actions by killing an animal or believing that someone else's death will pay our karmic debts.

The other meaning of the word sacrifice has to do with real life acts in which one person gives up their time, money, energy or even their life for someone else. In ancient times men went hunting to provide food for their family not knowing if they would return. My own father made this kind of sacrifice by going to work every day at a dangerous job that he hated so that his family could have the things they needed and wanted. Women sometimes sacrifice their careers to raise their families. Sometimes they make other sacrifices so that they can both raise a family and have a career. Real sacrifice requires that you place the welfare of others whom you love above your own or to quote Winston Churchhill, "We make a living by what we get; we make a life by what we give." As sons of the Horned God, we are called to make this kind of sacrifice. Spend some time thinking about the sacrifices that you are called to make.

Ritual offerings are closely related to ritual sacrifice though offerings don't usually involve the shedding of blood. In many Pagan religions, offerings are meant to honor the original sacrifices present throughout mythology. The sacrifice of the giant Ymir to create the Yggdrasil, the World Tree, is a prime example of such mythos. To honor this, ancient peoples would offer things that were essential to their survival such as food from the harvest, or tools they use in their trade. You might offer food, drink, flowers or incense to the Gods. In performing an offering, you are acknowledging these original sacrifices, as well as showing appreciation to the Gods for what they have provided you.

Cakes and ale is an example of an offering. Bread and wine is blessed and passed around the circle. It represents the gifts of the Goddess and the Horned God to us and our thankfulness for them. At the end of the walking meditation ritual you made an offering of an apple and water. The Samhain ritual in this book includes a libation offering in which you pour out the chalice of juice after toasting your ancestors. In other Samhain rituals I have fixed a plate of food for my ancestors, a custom referred to as the "mute supper." After the meal I left the ancestor's plate outside over night. When I was traveling in Vietnam last year I saw offerings of fruit, water and incense on altars in every home and hotel I visited. I understand that this is a Buddhist custom but it is one that we Pagans could adopt as a part of our daily worship of our Gods.

Consider what items might be appropriate to offer to a particular deity or spirit. Think carefully about the symbolism involved when you decide what to do with the offering after the ritual is over. Generally, liquids are poured out as libation, and food is left outside for animals as a symbolic honoring of deity. If you have done the rituals that you read about earlier in this book, you have made ritual some offerings. You are now ready to use offerings as part of the rituals that you write and as part of your daily spiritual practice.

Your Manhood Ritual

In our culture it is unusual for a young man to be recognized and treated as an adult while he is still in school whether this is high school or college. Therefore, I suggest that you delay your final rite of passage into manhood until after graduation but before you start your career. You have spent a number of years learning and practicing the skills and virtues you will need as a man. You have become proficient in camping in the wild. You have gone on a number of quests seeking to find out who you are, what your place is in the universe and be initiated by the Horned God and the Goddess. Your manhood ritual will be much like those other quests except that this time the purpose will be to return fully a man. If you are a part of a Pagan community the elder men should take charge of your rite. Otherwise you must take charge of your own rite.

Plan to spend a full year thinking about and planning your rite. Do not wait until the last minute when you will be studying for finals, involved in your graduation and trying to secure a position in your new career. Use all the resources at hand to find a location that is secluded and off the beaten path where you can be alone and not worry about being disturbed by other humans. You have by now been on quests before. You may choose a location in the same area as your previous quests, but don't pick the exact same spot. Look for a small hill that will give you a view of your surroundings. Take into account your health and safety. You want to come back from this a man not a corpse.

Let your parents know very early on what you plan to do and when. Whether or not you share the details as to why you are going will depend on how open you are about your spiritual path. Write each of them a letter that you will leave behind thanking them for being your parents and asking for a special meal to celebrate your return.

The basic form of the Manhood Ritual will be very similar to your other quest rituals. You will purify your body and set out for your destination. You will set up camp and establish sacred space. You will do walking and sitting meditations. You will pray to the Elements, the Horned God and the Goddess for a vision of who you are to be as a man. This time alone is the liminal phase of the ritual. There is an element of trial or testing involved in the isolation, fasting and prayer. You are prepared and you will pass the test. You will return changed by the experience.

When you have finished, it will be the time to celebrate and get some much needed rest. Break camp and know that you return home a man. During your next meal with your parents perhaps the opportunity will arise when you can share some of what you have learned and what your plans are for your future. Don't be surprised if you feel that something has changed. It has. In the days and years to come you will take your rightful place as a man among the men of your family and your tribe as a son of the Goddess and the Horned God. This is the reincorporation phase of your rite.

Afterword

Well, now what? That depends entirely on you, doesn't it? "You must choose... What you decide fates how you live and how you die."[25] Paganism is a path to be walked. It is not the correct path for everyone but it is the one I walk and perhaps the one you have chosen to walk. It is a path of hope. Hope for the individual and hope for the whole earth. If you choose to walk this path, take the first steps and the next and the next and then one day "we shall truly stand untouched by spear or scythe. We shall be the Oak and Holly. We will stand tall and guard Her, The Earth, as She sleeps."[26]

Bright blessings,
Dancing Rabbit
November 12, 2008

End Notes

1   Neil Chethik. "What should we do with the boys?" *UU World* XVII:1 (January/February 2003): pp. 28-32.

2   Jana Runnalls. "Spirit of the Cloven Hoof" http://www.sacredhome.co.uk. (accessed January 29, 2009).

3   Unitarian Universalist Association. "The Purposes of the Unitarian Universalist Association", http://www.uua.org/visitors/6798.shtml (accessed June 4, 2008).

4   Rev. Kendyl Gibbons. "Human Reverence." *UU World* XX:2 (Summer 2006): p. 37.

5   Unitarian Universalist Association. "The Purposes of the Unitarian Universalist Association", http://www.uua.org/visitors/6798.shtml (accessed June 4, 2008).

6   Unitarian Universalist Association. "The Purposes of the Unitarian Universalist Association", http://www.uua.org/visitors/6798.shtml (accessed June 4, 2008).

7   Nick Miller, email of March 29, 2007.

8   Traditional Native American, "Ancient Mother".

9   Kyri Comyn, "Charge of the Goddess", (Rocky Mountain Pagan Journal, 1986). Public Domain.

10 Dancing Rabbit. "Bloudewedd Chant", 2008.

11 Beth, Karen. "Full Moon Dance", *To Each of Us*, (Catkin Music).

12 Anonymous, "Cauldron of Change".

13 Silver on the Tree. "Cernunnos Chant", *Eye of Aeon*, (Silver Branch Productions, 1991. http://www.planetgong.co.uk/maze/blurbs/silverontree.shtml

14 Daniel Webster Christensen. "The Charge of the God", email of November 18, 2008.

[15] Fire Eagle, email of February 9, 2007.

[16] Dancing Rabbit. "By leaf and branch", 2009.

[17] Daniel Webster Christensen. "The Charge of the God", email of November 18, 2008.

[18] Buffalo. "Horned One, Lover, Son", *Welcome To Annwfn, Forever Forest*, (Sebastopol, CA: Serpentine Music Productions, 1986).

[19] Anonymous. "Old Ones Hear Us".

[20] Rudyard Kipling. "If...", (Project Gutenberg E-Book) Public Domain.

[21] Daniel Webster Christensen. "The Charge of the God", email of November 18, 2008.

[22] Daniel Webster Christensen. "The Charge of the God", email of November 18, 2008.

[23] Ravenlore, email of May 20, 2007.

[24] Jose Ballester. "The End of the Innocence", sermon delivered at 1st Unitarian Universalist Church of Houston, February 10, 2008.

[25] Daniel Webster Christensen. "The Charge of the God", email of November 18, 2008.

[26] Daniel Webster Christensen. "The Charge of the God", email of November 18, 2008.

Suggested Reading

Angeles, Ly De. *When I See the Wild God*. Llewellyn Publications, 2004.

Bonewits, Isaac. *The Pagan Man*. Citadel Press, 2005.

Drew, A. J. Wicca. *Spellcraft for Men*. New Page Books, 2001.

Drew, A. J. and Patricia Telesco. *God / Goddess*. Career Press, 2003.

Cuhulain, Kerr. *Full Contact Magick*. Llewellyn Publications, 2002.

Cuhulain, Kerr. *Wiccan Warrior*. Llewellyn Publications, 2000.

Cunningham, Scott. *Wicca: a guide for the solitary practitioner*. Llewellyn Publications, 2003.

Farrar, Janet and Stewart Farrar. *The Witches' God*. Phoenix Publishing, 1989.

Fitch, Eric L. *In Search of Herne the Hunter*. Capall Bann Publishing, 1994.

Foster, Steven. *The Book of the Vision Quest*. Simon & Schuster, 1992.

Morgan, Diane. *The Charmed Garden*. Findhorn Press, 2002.

Penczak, Christopher. *Sons of the Goddess*. Llewellyn, 2004.

Rey, A. J. *The Stars: a new way to see them*. Houghton Mifflin Company, 1980.

Starhawk. *The Spiral Dance*. Harper Collins, 1999.

West, Kate. *The Real Witches' Garden*. Element, 2004.